W9-CBH-447

Web Marketing for Small Businesses

7 Steps to Explosive Business Growth

Stephanie Diamond

SOURCEBOOKS, INC.
NAPERVILLE, ILLINOIS

DISCARDED
Shelton State Libraries
Shelton State Community College

Copyright © 2008 by Stephanie Diamond
Cover and internal design © 2008 by Sourcebooks, Inc.
Author photo by Whitney Lane, Lane Photography Studio
The Mind Maps used as illustrations in this book were created by using Mindjet MindManager. Mindjet and MindManager are registered trademarks of Mindjet Corporation. Sourcebooks and the colophon are registered trademarks of Sourcebooks, Inc.

All rights reserved. No part of this book may be reproduced in any form or by any electronic or mechanical means including information storage and retrieval systems—except in the case of brief quotations embodied in critical articles or reviews—without permission in writing from its publisher, Sourcebooks, Inc.

This publication is designed to provide accurate and authoritative information in regard to the subject matter covered. It is sold with the understanding that the publisher is not engaged in rendering legal, accounting, or other professional service. If legal advice or other expert assistance is required, the services of a competent professional person should be sought.—*From a Declaration of Principles Jointly Adopted by a Committee of the American Bar Association and a Committee of Publishers and Associations*

All brand names and product names used in this book are trademarks, registered trademarks, or trade names of their respective holders. Sourcebooks, Inc., is not associated with any product or vendor in this book.

Published by Sourcebooks, Inc.
P.O. Box 4410, Naperville, Illinois 60567-4410
(630) 961-3900
Fax: (630) 961-2168
www.sourcebooks.com

Library of Congress Cataloging-in-Publication Data

Diamond, Stephanie.
  Web marketing for small businesses : 7 steps to explosive business growth / Stephanie Diamond.
        p. cm.
  Includes bibliographical references.
  1. Internet marketing. I. Title.
  HF5415.1265.D53 2008
  658.8'72--dc22
                                    2008003916

Printed and bound in the United States of America
DR 10 9 8 7 6 5 4 3 2 1

To Barry, who makes all things possible
To my family, for their encouragement and love

Acknowledgments

I would like to offer my special gratitude and thanks to:

Those who made this book happen:
My agent Matt Wagner at Fresh Books
Editorial Trade Manager Peter Lynch and my talented editor Erin Nevius at
    Sourcebooks, Inc.

Those who generously contributed to my "Three Questions for the Experts"
    interviews:
Marc Barker (www.digmediaworks.com)
David Bascom (www.seo.com)
Mike Bell www.(software.com)
Chuck Frey (www.innovationtools.com)
Michael Harrison (www.roirevolution.com/blog)
Christine Kane (www.ChristineKane.com/blog)
Martin Middlewood (www.casestudy411.com)
Bob Morse (www.casestudy411.com)
Roger C. Parker (www.PublishedandProfitable.com)
Michael Stelzner (www.writingwhitepapers.com/blog)

My team at Digital Media Works, Inc. who continue to delight and amaze our
    customers:
Marc Barker
Rob Smith
Tony Jenkins
Marc Bostian
Paul Ferree

My super smart colleagues at Mindjet for their creativity:
Linda Cleary
Melinda Venable
Gaelen O'Connell
Kymberly Shannon

And thanks to all my colleagues who elevate my thinking on a daily basis.

Contents

Section 1

What's New Online

Chapter

What's Important to Today's Web Marketer?

The best way to predict the future is to create it.
—Peter Drucker

- ▶ Make It Easy to Tell Your Story
- ▶ Social Media Marketing—A Definition
- ▶ Who is the Audience for Social Media Marketing?
- ▶ A Look Back at How We Got Here
- ▶ Marketing of the Future
- ▶ Web Developments that Made a Difference
- ▶ Tactics You Should Consider

Shelton State Libraries
Shelton State Community College

We are a nation of storytellers—and we are an attentive audience. From reality shows to political blogs to home videos, we secretly love to watch someone else's drama unfold from the safety of our living room. And with the rise of internet technology, we can instantly share these stories with everyone around the globe. As reporter Thomas Friedman says, the world is flat—there are no boundaries or limits.

Make It Easy to Tell Your Story

I'm sure you've heard many times that the key to creating a successful business on the Web is choosing the right tactics and delivering your message to the right audience. But there is a secret, something that will help you be more successful than you might otherwise be. The secret is that you need to make it easy for people to tell *your* story.

Web 2.0 has made it possible for people to share stories with anyone who will sit in front of a computer screen, and these people are looking for stories to tell to their audience. Shouldn't it be your story? Why couldn't it be your story? Couldn't you help them spread the word about the value of your products and services?

When I started Digital Media Works, Inc., my online marketing and design business, in 2002, I decided my tagline would be "Make it Easy to Buy." At that time, just getting through an online transaction was a major triumph for most consumers. But now this slogan has new meaning.

The Web has left its infancy; we're in the teen years, where consumers control and shape your brand. With the rise of customer control, everyone delights in telling stories, via podcasts, videos, blogs, etc., about their experiences with a company or product. Therefore, a businessperson's number one job is to make it easy for people on the web to tell compelling stories about your company.

Social Media Marketing—A Definition

Throw out what you know about Social Media Marketing (SMM) and start this book with a fresh perspective. There is a lot of bad information and just plain wrong information about SMM out there. Also, and it's changing at the speed of light, and new information is constantly being added. For that reason, let's nail down a working definition we'll use throughout the book. Simply put, **SMM is marketing that focuses on people, not products**. You want to focus your attention on tactics that help you create a conversation with your customer. As the authors Rick Levine, Christopher Locke, Doc Searls, and David Weinberger set forth in *The Cluetrain Manifesto*, written in 1999, "markets are conversations."

Wikipedia.com says that the goals for SMM "will differ for every business or organization, however most will involve some form of building an idea or brand awareness, increase visibility, encouraging brand feedback and dialogue as well as to possibly sell a product or service. SMM may also include online reputation management." There is much disagreement about what SMM really means. Robert Scoble, best known for his blog Scobelizer.com, takes a shot at defining social media. He says, "the best way to understand a new media is to compare it to what's come before." When you look at old media you find things like newspapers, magazines, radio, CDs, etc. The similarity among all of those is the inability to modify them once they are published. With social media, you can modify and combine in new ways. When you market using social media, you are providing media to a specific targeted social network. You are encouraging the users of that network to interact and share the information.

Today, marketing choices are endless—you can set up a Facebook page, record podcasts, create RSS feeds, and publish your own newsletter all before lunch. But how many of these new tactics really apply to you and your business? When colleagues ask if you're using the latest cool tool, you sigh and say no—but you don't need to use every marketing tool available to you to be effective. With all the possibilities and venues of marketing these days, you need to determine what will work best for you. Without a step-by-step plan to evaluate each tool and integrate them into your campaigns, you'll waste valuable time.

QUICK Tip

Approach any new marketing strategy or tactic with a healthy dose of skepticism. Ask yourself one important question: "Will it help increase revenue and grow my business?" If the answer is yes, explore different ways of applying it. If the answer is no, wait and see. As a businessperson, you want to see if specific tactics have any real upside for you. Let a new website or online marketing tool have the time to prove itself useful and cost effective before you jump in.

Alert!

What are people searching for online? A look at the top searches on Google from the U.S. in April of 2007 shows the types of information people are looking for online (Hitwise, 2007):

- Health and medical, 29 percent
- Travel, 20 percent
- Shopping and classified, 16 percent
- News and media, 13 percent
- Entertainment, 13 percent
- Business and finance, 10 percent

If you are selling products in any of these fields, an eager audience is searching for you.

Who is the Audience for Social Media Marketing?

Nielsen/Net Ratings classifies the group most likely to use social networking sites as "My.Internet." A study they conducted in 2006 showed that 16 percent of all Web users are part of this group and their average age is thirty-two (no one under eighteen was surveyed).

What does their online activity look like?

- 99 percent visit blogs
- 84 percent belong to an online community
- 57 percent have their own blog
- 22 percent use RSS fccds

AdvertisingAge.com reports that more than 22 percent of eighteen- to twenty-four-year-olds are watching less TV now that they use social networking sites like Facebook and MySpace.

Figure 1.1: WEB USERS BY GENERATION

A 2006 study by Forrester Research found the following information about generational use of the web.

Gen Y, ages eighteen to twenty-six

- This group spends an average of 12.2 hours a week online.
- Up to 40 percent say they like to "research products online and purchase offline."

Gen X, ages twenty-seven to forty

- This group spends 28 percent less time online than Gen Y.

Boomers, ages forty-one to sixty-one

- Less than 30 percent of young boomers (forty-one to fifty) report checking stocks online and sending photos via email.
- Less than 25 percent of older boomers (fifty-one to sixty) research online and buy offline. The majority will research and buy online.
- The International Herald Tribune reports that there are approximately 78 million boomers, which is three times the number of teenagers and twenty-somethings.

Seniors, ages sixty-two and over

- This group leads all other groups in checking stocks online and receiving photos via email.

- An interesting study by Third Age and JWT Boom of Internet users aged forty-five and up found that 73 percent list shopping online as one of their favorite online activities. Sharon Whitely, CEO of Third Age, is quoted as saying, "The conventional wisdom that Boomers and mid-lifers are set in their purchasing habits and resistant to marketing messages is a very costly myth."

Benefits to your Business

In a global survey by the McKinsey management consulting firm in March 2007 called "How Businesses are Using Web 2.0," they cite the benefits of online marketing to their organizations as:

- the ability to engage the customer in dialogue
- the reduction of churn rate (customer turnover) because of blogs and RSS feeds which
- the ability to satisfy the customer and cause him to increase his loyalty
- the option of using customer opinions and expertise to improve product design

There are six ways new online developments can benefit your business. You can:

1. Interact with the entire world, no limits.
2. Measure everything.
3. Create joint ventures very easily.
4. Let your customers contribute content that adds value to your company.
5. Let your customers join together to create a new product.
6. Employ the "Long-Tail" business model.

QUICK Tip

Long-Tail Marketing: Chris Anderson, editor in chief of *Wired* Magazine, first described the theory of the "Long-Tail business model" as it applied to entertainment markets. In essence, the theory states that the future of the entertainment business lies in its ability to target millions of niche markets; that businesses with powerful distribution (such as on the Web) will do better selling small, hard-to-find items than expensive, popular ones.

This theory, of course, has application for all businesses with an online presence. Online, people use very specific search phrases to find a narrowly defined topic of interest. You have to know what your niche market is and tailor your message and website to them.

A Look Back at How We Got Here

No company is immune from online scrutiny, and everyone has an opinion. Consider the plight of Comcast. How many people watched the 2006 YouTube video of the Comcast technician sleeping on his customer's couch? (You can view it at http://www.youtube.com/watch?v= CvVp7b5 gzqU.) It is an entertaining video that tells story—not a great story—about Comcast's service and work ethic.

To understand how this constant and immediate feedback affects your business today, let's take a quick look back at some of the highlights of advertising. I think it's important to have this historical perspective because without it, it's hard to understand the enormous role the Web has played in changing the game.

The '50s

Pre-Internet, marketers in the mid-twentieth century had few very specific advertising choices—they were fairly limited to one or a combination of television, radio, direct mail, sponsorships, and billboards. Marketers would run focus groups and hope they could capture the thoughts and feelings of customers and satisfy their needs based on the opinions of these groups. It may have looked scientific, but immediate feedback was limited.

Basically, marketers in the 1950s took their best shot and hoped they guessed right. Some advertising was entertaining but showed no return. Some advertising made no impact at all, while others were wildly successful. There was a lack of accurate data that actually told you how effective your campaign was, and the process was inefficient and inexact.

CASE STUDY: Advertising in the '50s

In the 1950s, companies would sponsor entire shows, so you would watch the Colgate Comedy Hour and hear about their products during commercial breaks. A company could have a say in the content of the program, and threaten to pull their sponsorship if they didn't like what was planned. This gave advertisers almost total control. The goods were limited and the message was one-way—the products were forced upon consumers, who had very few ways to give feedback.

John Wanamaker, Philadelphia department store magnate, was famously quoted as saying, "I know half my advertising is wasted. I just don't know which half."

The '60 and '70s

Next came the '60s and '70s. This era was marked by regulation and social upheaval. We were in a race to the moon with Russia, and in 1964, cigarettes were deemed hazardous to your health and most magazines banned their advertising. Social mores began changing in the late '60s and music and politics were having a great impact on everything, including advertising. In 1971 the National Advertising Review board was created to look into issues of taste and social responsibility. As a consequence of this, advertisers wanted to steer clear of controversy and entertain their audiences—lots of the advertising was funny and clever. Some of it produced results, some didn't. Controversy was kept to a minimum. The era closed with big corporations controlling the style of advertising. In 1974, the top three corporations spending the most money on advertising were Procter & Gamble, General Foods, and Bristol-Myers. These corporations sought very little feedback from consumers. It was a one-way street.

The '80s and '90s

Then came the '80s and '90s and their "conspicuous consumerism": people wore the names of the brands they preferred as conspicuously as possible, and advertisers climbed over themselves to make their product cool and hip. People bought brands they believed gave them status. In the movie *Back to the Future* (1985), audiences laughed in recognition when one of the characters called Michael J. Fox's character "Calvin Klein." He said, "That is your name, isn't it? Calvin Klein? It's written all over your underwear." The '80s and '90s were actually very good to marketers and advertisers—they knew they were doing something right if they saw their brand displayed by lots of people. It was immediate feedback.

Marketing of the Future

By the late 1990s the mood was beginning to shift. "Interruption marketing" was declared dead by a host of online marketers, although offline marketers still employed it. Interruption marketing is the method by which advertisers interrupt whatever is happening on your TV, radio, or other broadcast channels to deliver their message, whether you want to hear it or not. It's a seventy-plus-year-old advertising model, and it's due for retirement.

With the advent of the Web, a new model was possible. Marketing expert Seth Godin called it "Permission Marketing" in his book of the same name. However, it was not adopted on the spot. It evolved based on technological improvements from Web 2.0 and the growing control of the audience.

Fear of the unknown

In the early days of the Web, online marketing was a very small adjunct to whatever "real" marketing a company was doing. Some were successful with their online efforts; some were not. This inconsistency engendered more fear, and people were afraid to venture onto the Internet.

CASE STUDY: Branching Out

In my tenure at AOL, which started in 1994, I worked with some companies who were afraid to create a website. They saw it as the Wild West—lots of unknowns for "who knows what" return. Watching these companies make their way through unknown territory and build a website was exciting—it was complex, and the technology was constantly changing.

Fast forward to today. Everyone including your dry cleaner and local take-out joint has a website; the customer reach it affords makes it imperative for almost every business to be online. People email their lunch orders to the local diner and pick them up at noon. It's the first place consumers go to research products, find new things to do, and connect with other people.

The Web has begun an era of consumer control. People decide whether they want to view a commercial (TiVo), get a phone call from a marketer at dinnertime (the "do not call" list), or see a pop-up ad (pop-up blockers). Consumers have made it clear that their time is too valuable to be wasted. They are overwhelmed by job duties and family responsibilities. Their free time is very limited, and they have the tools at their disposal to make sure it is not wasted.

Alert!

The new market: There has been a paradigm shift in marketing, a transfer of power. Not only do customers want to be asked permission by marketers; they want to actively engage in and participate in the product conversation. People want to tell you what they think, how they view your brand, and how you can improve. This information can not only improve your products and services, but it can increase customer satisfaction and get people to tell your story.

Much has been made of storytelling in the twenty-first century. Now the story becomes one that you have to not only make appealing to your customer—you also have to make it easy for the customer to tell that story to all their friends. That means you need to change your job description. Think about it.

Experience Matters: Your focus today must be on the total customer experience if you are to create a meaningful brand. Now more than ever, this experience is the new currency that interests people.

People used to aspire to the good life—they saved and planned in order to, one day, be able to afford all the finer things in life. But nowadays, it's all about "experiencing" the good life, no long-term commitment required. You can lease the car of your dreams, rent a yacht, take trendy luxury vacations, and wear all manner of designer duds on loan. This trend has been making its way to a tipping point. It's really important for small business owners to take note and satisfy this need for instant gratification.

Web Developments that Made a Difference

Marketers are struggling to adjust to the shift in power brought on by the advent of Web 2.0. Stanford Law professor Lawrence Lessig distinguishes Web 2.0 content as "writeable." What he means by that is the content can be reshaped and shared to make it better, unlike Web 1.0 where the message was one-way. Whether they like it or not, today's marketers can't dictate when you'll hear a message or what you'll do with it. Previously, shoppers were limited to whatever goods and services they could find in their local area. Now, the Internet provides a limitless array. You can sit down in front of your computer and find whatever your heart desires.

How did this shift happen? What turned passive consumers into active participants? To understand it, let's look at how new web technologies changed the online business landscape.

At the beginning of the digital age, websites conducted a one-way conversation with their visitors. Marketers would post content talking about their company, their products, and their awards. Users would go online, look at the material, and buy based on what they learned about the product.

Fast forward to Web 2.0. New technology has made it possible for users to speak to other users, completely bypassing the website owner. This takes the power out of the owner's hands and puts it into the consumer's hands. In 2005, Tim O'Reilly, founder of computer book publisher O'Reilly Media, coined the phrase "Web 2.0" and produced a paper entitled "What is Web 2.0." It looked at some of the things that shaped the next generation of web technology. The use of Web 2.0 tools fostered a change in the way businesses interact with customers. Customers now have the power to shop from an unlimited supply of vendors. If they don't like the price or service, they can quickly find a replacement. Business owners can no longer take customers for granted. They need to listen to customers and follow up.

Alert!

The new availability: As with TV, people can go online anytime. But, unlike broadcast TV, there is no set schedule. You can log into your favorite auto supply store at one o'clock in the afternoon or one o'clock in the morning. It all looks and functions exactly the same. This frees the consumer to shop and surf when it's convenient for them. The battle cry, "what you want, when you want it," echoes through the canyons of Madison Avenue.

A study by Jupiter Research in January 2006 found that online users spend as much time online in a week as they do watching TV, about fourteen hours. The study reports that for "a large segment of the American public, the Internet is now the most important broadcast medium." In October 2007, AdvertisingAge.com reported that "almost 29 percent of the twelve- to sixty-four-year-old population say that the PC is competing with the TV for their entertainment time…and 15 percent say they watch less TV as a result of watching online videos."

The Web vs. TV: When Ted Leonsis (currently Vice Chairman of AOL), would attend conferences to speak about ISPs in the 1990s, he would say that they were not competing with each other, they were competing with *Seinfeld*. Over ten years later, it looks like the Web is winning, or at least it's a fight among equals.

So what new developments were fostered by this new generation of technology and its savvy users? We've seen the rise of eight business practices that did not substantially exist before Web 2.0:

1. Online marketing as an expressed preference

Online shopping is quick and easy—many people prefer it, so marketers are spending more money to reach an online audience. In 1994, no one had a budget for online advertising. Now online ad spending is a routine part of the mix.

In 2007, when JCPenney's CEO Mike Ullman was asked how much of their $1 billion ad budget was allocated online, he replied: "Not much. We're still mostly direct mail." So, while not every retailer participates, by and large online ad spending continues to grow.

2. User-generated content

User-generated content (UGC, also known as consumer-generated media) is one of the hallmarks of social media. It is online content created by and for users. You find new UGC in blogs, wikis, videos, podcasts, and discussion groups every day. A 2007 Pew Research study on "Home Broadband Adoption," reports that over 48 million American adults (35 percent of U.S. Internet users) have created and posted content online.

Users can express what they think and offer opinions on just about anything online; this ability has changed the world and the face of business. Some of the most well-known of these types of websites are YouTube, MySpace, and Facebook. (More about these sites in Chapter 13.)

QUICK Tip

User-Generated Content: The Organization for Economic Cooperation and Development (OECD) says that UGC has three characteristics: (1) it has to be published somewhere online; (2) it needs to have creative effort put into it; and (3) it needs to be something that was not created as part of a job. An obvious example would be a YouTube video created just for entertainment. In UGC you can find debate, thoughtful expressions, misinformation, and downright hostile rants.

A marketing management survey by PRWeek and the Word of Mouth Marketing Association found that 31 percent of people who used UGC and based some purchases on it did so because of the "declining credibility of traditional advertising." However, the survey found there is some hesitation by marketers to use it. Some 32 percent of marketers don't use UGC because "there's no clear ROI." Another 6 percent cite the fact that they don't want to have such a close tie to their consumers, and 33 percent cite other reasons like, "we've had difficulty in getting the establishment to understand it."

3. Collective user intelligence

Once you have the technical capability to generate user content, you also have the opportunity to make that content stronger and more complete by allowing users to add, subtract, and enhance. For example, when you visit Wikipedia.com, you see an online encyclopedia whose English language version contains more than two million entries. Volunteers submitted these entries and then collectively corrected and enhanced them. Other well-known examples are bookmarking sites like Digg and Flickr. This capability has the potential to enhance any company that has users who could contribute to their knowledge base in some way.

4. Collaboration

What comes to mind when you think about business collaboration? You probably visualize several people sitting around a conference table looking at a white board. In today's world of online collaboration, that's just a sliver of what you could be doing. Today, you can use wikis, blogs, and social networking sites to open up the collaborative flow and get information from everywhere.

Previously, marketers would expect customers to buy into the definition of their brand without getting customer feedback. Marketers would still love to apply this model, but it's no longer possible. Now that consumers can easily talk to other consumers, the information flows back and forth.

There are two groups you need to think about when planning online collaboration efforts:

- Customers and other interested third parties. They can shape the meaning of a brand and sell it to others. According to a 2007 McKinsey Global survey, 22 percent of the companies surveyed say they host user forums so that customers can support one another and share product information. Two-thirds use them to involve their customers in product development. It's important for marketers to respect this collaboration. If consumers get wind of the notion that something is a pure marketing ploy and not a sincere attempt to collaborate, the backlash is tremendous.
- Employees around the world. Aside from the difference in time zone, employees can work together easily online to share and grow their company's vision.

CASE STUDY: Xerox dreams with the customer

To stay competitive, Xerox has begun collaborating with their customers. For many years, Xerox had no competition in the world of photocopying, but now they risk losing customers to Canon, IBM, and Kodak. So Xerox created a brainstorming process called "dreaming with the customer" to get insight into real customer desires.

When their engineers were in the process of developing a new printer, they had the idea to create one with two engines, thinking the second engine could be used for specialized inks and colors. They presented this idea to groups of customers via eight online conferences. When one of the customers heard the idea, he was excited that if one of the engines went down, they could still use the second while they waited for service. The customers all agreed this could be great. The idea sent shockwaves through the engineers; they thought they knew what the user wanted, but when they actually spoke to them, they found that they really didn't have the full picture.

If you've ever worked in a big company, you know this attitude is a huge turnaround. And for small business owners, listening and collaborating is a necessity. It's easier now than it has ever been to have an advisory group of customers to tell you how they use your products and what else they might need. If the big companies are doing it, you can do it better.

5. The growth of "influencers"

At no time in our history has it ever been easier to share our opinion with someone around the block or around the world. With the growing introduction of social media tools, marketers are now able to impact word-of-mouth (WOM) marketing more successfully. Word-of-mouth is immediate and less costly than focus groups and large studies. It is solicited from friends and associates, making it targeted and personal. It puts control in customers' hands—if someone doesn't like your product, they can make sure that everyone knows it. They may also be able to see the effects of their negative review. (For more detailed information on this topic, see Chapter 17.)

6. Rapid prototyping and quick outcomes

Forrester Research analyst Josh Bernoff is quoted as saying, "If you looked at a marketing initiative five years ago, it involved a whole lot of planning and expense...now it's about coming up with an idea and taking three weeks to implement." Starting a business is easier than ever before. The greatest benefit of this is that it doesn't take long for you to determine whether your idea is viable.

7. Real-time meetings

The development of real-time meetings has been a tremendous boon to companies who can't afford or don't want the hassle of sending their employees on long business trips. With the annoyances that go with plane travel today, business travelers are breathing a sigh of relief when they can conduct sales meetings and conferences online. Companies such as GoToMeeting.com and WebEx provide an easy way for people to gather around their own monitors and discuss a project or sales initiative.

8. Social networking

A comScore report found that social networking traffic increased 774 percent between June 2006 and June 2007. Facebook's daily visitation alone increased 299 percent. For businesses, social networks like LinkedIn have grown substantially. According to Nielsen Ratings, LinkedIn grew 189 percent from October 2006 to October 2007. This is significant because it starts to level the playing field for executives who did not have large offline social networks to turn to for referrals. By networking with colleagues online, you can grow your network and expand your business, and you can meet people you would not normally have access to. One well-known entrepreneur spoke about how she landed a magazine column by networking only with people on LinkedIn.

Tactics You Should Consider

What are some of the social media tactics you should be thinking about adding to your website? We look at them briefly here, and in depth later in Chapter 13.

Reviews and recommendations

Having customer reviews on your site can be a scary thought—after all, the goal of marketing is usually to share only positive information. However, if there is a problem, you want to know about it as soon as possible. Getting negative feedback is better than having sales dry up unexpectedly.

 **With or without you:** Given online shopping today, people will seek out opinions and reviews of your products, on or off your site. That's what search engines are for. Having them on your site is not risky unless your product is mediocre and your service is bad. Personally, I have often declined to purchase products with bad reviews, but more often than not I've read through the list of comments and found a give and take that helps you make a decision, and not always a negative one.

Forums

These can take the form of tips and troubleshooting information shared among customers. It drives satisfaction and a sense of community. It will also help you cut back on customer service calls if the forum identifies a problem and provides steps on how to correct it. This can also help you generate other content like help videos and posts on how to handle problems.

Video and photo sharing

Find a place on your site for customer photos or videos. One way to encourage customers to send these is to have a contest and ask customers to send in a picture of themselves along with their entry. This can be beneficial in two ways: you can post the winning entries and have interesting, consumer-generated info on your site, and the contest might generate some good ideas for you. Newsletter contests are fun and easy, and a winner can be featured in each issue.

In this chapter we looked at technology that made a difference. In the next chapter we see how this technology has changed the roles of marketers and consumers.

Chapter

Changing Roles

Change is the process by which the future invades our lives.

—*Alvin Toffler*

Clearly, new technology changes the way marketers and customers interact. Tim O'Reilly, whose team coined the term Web 2.0, called it the "architecture of participation." The user is no longer just a consumer of media—he is a participant. He doesn't sit back and wait for the message to wash over him. He can tag and vote on content and bookmark sites for others to find.

Change Your Job Description

The role of the online business owner continues to change as new web tools become available. This makes it key to have everyone who works for you willing to change their job description in order to get the biggest return from your marketing efforts. Instead of viewing themselves as sales people, customer service techs, or accounting experts, they need to see their role as making it easy for the customer to come away with a great story about the company that they can tell their friends and family.

This change can cause your profits to climb without a drastic change in organization. Everyone must look at the task at hand, determine how their actions can satisfy the customer, and prompt the customer to tell others about that satisfaction. This is a deceptively simple idea, but don't skip over it—it can breathe a new life and focus into your company that is invaluable.

The New Role of the Consumer

The buyer's new mindset is one in which they, as a consumer:

- Listen to advertising on their own terms. What you want, when you want it—DVRs that save television programs for later viewing, TiVos that cut out commercials, and pop-up blockers that avoid ads.
- Are in control of the buying process. Now that they have the freedom to search for products and talk to other consumers, potential buyers can't be spoon-fed only the information marketers want them to have.
- Drive the personality of the brand. Consumers decide what the real meaning of a company's brand is and drive the popularity—or lack thereof.
- Join with other consumers to enhance the product itself. Enthusiasts of a brand can band together and share information, help design new products, and encourage others to try the product.

The New Role of the Marketer

In response to the change in customer mindset, here are some changes you, as a marketer, should consider:

- Be authentic and demonstrate your values in everything you present to the customer.
- Respect the customer's opinion, and show that you do.
- Make it easy for customers to share your brand stories with others.
- Make sure your employees love your brand; their passion will be contagious, as will their displeasure.
- Understand the extent to which your brand evokes strong feelings or provides a special experience. Listen to your customer's passion and don't cling to the false belief that you can dictate what they feel for very long.
- Try to make everything about the customer experience special, from the packing slip to the unexpected freebies you throw in the box. Pay attention to each part of the experience and continue to make it better.
- Lead your company by listening to the voice of your customers.
- Don't expect success if you run your company with old marketing notions about how to "sell" and what to measure. Sometimes social media marketing tools don't produce an immediate ROI.

Figure 2.1: TWENTY-FIRST CENTURY SKILLS

Claudia Wallis and Sonja Steptoe's article in *Time* in December of 2006, "How to Bring Our Schools out of the Twentieth Century," gave advice to students that could just as easily be applied to the twenty-first century entrepreneur or small business owner. Their role has changed drastically, and they need to adapt.

Wallis and Steptoe list the twenty-first century skills as:

- Knowing more about the world—Web 2.0 technology makes borders and boundaries less relevant to the small business owner. An awareness of how this impacts business is essential.

- Thinking outside the box—In the new economy, creativity and innovation are prized skills. Every online business owner knows that the ground shifts beneath him on a regular basis. Learning to make that work for you is key.

- Becoming smarter about new sources of information—We have more information available to us now than ever before, but can we make sense of it? If you don't, you can feel overwhelmed. Besides having new sources of information, you need to have ways to effectively interpret and apply that information.

- Developing good people skills—Okay, this one may surprise you. People skills have always been an important skill, why the emphasis now? Collaboration and teamwork has become critical to working on Web 2.0. The ability to understand and work with people from other cultures has become critical.

The New Role of the Business Owner

The business owner has one more new role in the twenty-first century, and that is to *simplify* whenever and wherever possible—simplify products for customers, simplify processes for employees and vendors. Make it easy to do complex things. People are overwhelmed by information, tasks, and activities. They will respond positively to anything that attempts to simplify something they need to deal with.

Alert!

The need for simplicity: With regard to my work in online marketing, I have long been an advocate of making things easier—breaking things down into smaller chunks, saving time and money. Anyone who deals with technology yearns for simplicity.

In his elegant and slim volume, *The Laws of Simplicity*, John Maeda presents ten laws that he believes encapsulate what simplicity is. Here are the first five to help you think about integrating simplicity:

1. Reduce—the fastest way to achieve simplicity is through thoughtful reduction.
2. Organize—a system of many thoughtful steps appears simpler.
3. Time—savings in time feel like simplicity.
4. Learn—knowledge makes everything simpler.
5. Differences—simplicity and complexity need each other.

QUICK Tip

Tone it down: As you approach every thing you do online, always ask yourself, "how can I simplify this?" Some possible areas to start simplifying:

- website navigation
- long product descriptions
- ways of redeeming online offers
- information presentation
- product and service design

Customer feedback will prove very helpful here. The best way to make things easier is to ask people who use it what they find hard or confusing.

What Social Media Tools are Marketers Using?

In 2007, Paul Dunay, author of the Buzz Marketing for Technology Blog at http://buzzmarketingfortech.blogspot.com/, and Robert Lesser of Direct Impact Marketing, Inc., conducted a survey of marketers to determine which Web 2.0 technology they used.

They found that the top five media most commonly used are:

- Blogs, 64 percent
- RSS, 58 percent
- Podcasts, 54 percent
- Videocasts, 43 percent
- Social networks/communities, 42 percent

The Most Value from 2.0: Interestingly, a report released in July 2007 from Forrester Research, an independent technology and market research company, reports that 23 percent of businesses surveyed said that RSS has the most substantial business value to them among Web 2.0 technologies. Podcasting was behind it at 21 percent. Even more interestingly, 11 percent said they do not measure Web 2.0 business value at all.

However, there is another, even more pressing reason to get involved in Web 2.0 technology—your employees are going to do it with or without your consent or knowledge. Wouldn't you rather have a hand in it? Market research firm IDC conducted a research survey that showed that without company knowledge:

- 45 percent of companies have workers blogging
- 43 percent of companies have workers that use RSS feeds
- 33 percent of companies have workers using wikis

You could harness all this manpower and make it work for you.

Companies also need to participate in Web 2.0 because it is increasingly how they find and attract newly college-graduated employees. Businesses have to employ these technologies so that potential younger employees will be convinced that the company is forward thinking enough to use these tools.

New Role for Your Website

Let's get specific and look at exactly what kinds of tactics you need to employ on your website or other online marketing channels to support this role transition. It's easy to say "value your customer's opinion" or "let your customer's voice guide you." It's harder to put that into practice. What you need to do is look at the website tools available to you and decide which ones would be best to add to boost your customer satisfaction.

An April 2007 study by the J. C. Williams Group (in partnership with StartSampling and the E-tailing group), called "Transforming the Multichannel Shopper" asked users to list what they felt to be the most "helpful online features and tools." At the top of the list was customer reviews, cited by 92 percent of respondents.

Users went on to rate tools and features in order of helpfulness. This list can be used as a checklist to help you determine which of the most important social media features and tools to include on your website. Check off the ones you think you'd like to try.

Figure 2.2: CHECKLIST OF WEBSITE FEATURES AND TOOLS

Voted for by 92–54%	Yes	No	Voted for by 51–31%	Yes	No
Customer reviews			Recently viewed products		
Keyword search			What's new section		
Store locator			Customized content		
Product comparison			Related/recommended products		
Zoom/rotate			Live chat		
Catalog quick order			Wish list		
Clickable catalog			Audio or video clips		
Order history			Top sellers listing		
Loyalty program			Gift suggestions		
Alternative product reviews			Discussion board/blogs		

*Statistics obtained from April 2006 study called "Transforming the Multichannel Shopper," prepared by J. C. Williams Group in partnership with StartSampling and the E-tailing Group.

Think Like Amazon

Now that you've checked off the features and tools you think would make your site more valuable, let's look at an example of a site that has made use of all of these tools and features: Amazon.com. It's the world's biggest retail store on the Web, and it makes use of the top features most people find helpful—and that's no accident.

In order to think like Amazon does, you need to put yourself in the shoes of its founder, Jeff Bezos, in 2002. His company had developed an enormous proprietary database online that held information, reviews, pricing, etc., on books, movies, and more. Most people would consider it the lifeline of the business—all that data and feedback in one place. Bezos gambled that by opening up his database to developers, the company would grow stronger. His gamble proved correct. He let developers use Amazon's infrastructure to build new, more powerful shopping venues of their own. This ties their success to Amazon's.

I use this illustration to show you that allowing customers and vendors to share in the growth of your business can be done. Of course, you need to tread carefully and not expose yourself to unnecessary risk. But at least open your mind to the idea.

CASE STUDY: Amazon.com's features

Note that the list of features that Amazon uses to provide their customers with a better shopping experience is exactly the same as the list in Figure 2.2. This is not an accident. They have focused on extending the features that have clearly had a positive impact on their revenue.

- *Customer reviews*
- *Keyword search*
- *Store locator (it's an online store, but they partner with offline stores and provide locators)*
- *Product comparison*
- *Zoom/rotate—not available*

- *Catalog/quick order*
- *Clickable catalog*
- *Order history*
- *Loyalty program*
- *Alternative product reviews*
- *Recently viewed items*
- *What's New section*
- *Customized content*
- *Related/recommended products*
- *Live chat*
- *Wish list*
- *Audio or video clips*
- *Top sellers listing*
- *Gift suggestions*
- *Discussion board/blogs*

Section II
A New Mindset

Chapter

Creativity and Innovation

The important thing is to not stop questioning.
—Albert Einstein

- ▶ **Why Does Creativity Matter?**
- ▶ **How Does Being Creative Benefit Your Business?**
- ▶ **Seven Tips for Fostering Creativity**
- ▶ **Mind Mapping**

Why discuss a topic like creativity in a book about web marketing? The answer is simple. We are living in an era that prizes conceptual thinking and creativity, and good small businesses appear online and zoom to dramatic heights quicker than you can say MySpace. You need to position yourself to be able to take advantage of the new ways of seeing and creating that the Web is opening.

Why Does Creativity Matter?

Daniel Pink said in his 2005 groundbreaking book, *A Whole New Mind*, that "the 'right-brain' qualities of inventiveness, empathy, joyfulness and meaning—increasingly will determine who flourishes and who flounders." You need to be able to make the most of your talents and skills in these areas in order to succeed in business today.

Alert!

It is widely believed that people are naturally creative, but that as we develop and go through school, our creativity is discouraged and it atrophies. To grow your new business, you need to reawaken your creativity.

Let's start by looking at how you might be prevented from reaching your business goals if you do not encourage your creativity. In his book, *The War of Art*, Steven Pressfield concludes that there is only one thing that prevents people from achieving their dreams. He calls it resistance. You face resistance in the form of fear, envy, negative self-talk, and "helpful" comments from friends.

Essentially, to overcome resistance, you need to follow your own intuition. I'm confident that you can think of five reasons why you shouldn't try a new business idea or product. Most of them are probably reasonable—they may not be true, but they are reasonable. That's resistance. To overcome resistance you need to rely on your intuition, your belief that you know what's best for your company. Creativity can help you overcome that resistance.

How Does Being Creative Benefit Your Business?

Small business owners have the advantage of being nimble enough to quickly respond to shifts in the online marketplace. But what direction should you choose? You need to prepare for the next new product or service that will create new customers in the future. If you believe that you can wait until that product is in the marketplace and adapt it, you are missing the boat. Author and innovator Geoffrey Moore was quoted in 2006 in *CIO Magazine* as saying, "If you allocate all your resources based on your revenue makers or margin makers, you're driving in the rearview mirror." You want to be ready for the next wave of innovation. That's why you need to foster your own creativity.

Creativity helps you:

- Determine your company vision and purpose
- Deal with swift changes
- Find new niches and product ideas
- Increase your productivity
- Balance your work/home life

CASE STUDY: Brainstorming works

Businessweek columnist and marketing guru Doug Hall reported on an interesting survey he conducted at his Eureka! Ranch in 2007. He studied how small and medium-sized companies grew based on how they used their new ideas. The results were intriguing. Those who brainstormed and worked on many ideas for growth grew 5.8 times faster than those with only a few options. This is counterintuitive, since we usually hear that too many choices can cause confusion and inaction.

His study showed that having a wealth of ideas caused small businesses to flourish and employees to be more optimistic about the future. Creativity and new ideas help your company grow. If you only have one new idea you may convince yourself it's good. If you have several, you can afford to throw some out and rework them until they're great.

Innovation is something that needs to lead to real products and services. Part of your time and money should be spent on figuring out how your products will evolve. This does not mean chasing the next big thing. It means carefully analyzing your strategy and developing your business plan to serve you in the future.

Uncover your "genius" style

Can you nurture your creativity? How do you analyze your creative strengths? The first step is to figure out your "genius" style.

When David Galenson, author of *Old Masters and Young Geniuses*, was interviewed in the July 2007 issue of *Wired*, he said there were two types of creativity—quick and dramatic or careful and quiet. Galenson, a professor and economist, conducted a detailed study of well-known artists, writers, and film-makers. He found that their "genius" fell into one of two groups. They either did their best work at a very young age, like Pablo Picasso, or in their later years, like Frank Lloyd Wright. Late bloomers rejoice!

He called those who peaked early "Conceptualists" and those who peaked later "Experimentalists." He believes that this theory can be applied to business people as well. This can help you begin to understand your own innovation style. Conceptualists know what they want and proceed in a straight line until they find it. Experimentalists succeed through trial and error and almost never feel they have come to the end of their search. I'm sure one of these styles is familiar to you. You are either the slow, steady type who makes progress carefully or the one who takes risks and learns best from his own mistakes.

Both styles are equally potent, so you should feel entitled to do things your way. Some business owners find the one right solution and stick with it. Other are constantly revising and changing. Also, once you understand your own style it will be easier for you to manage your staff and their styles.

Seven Tips for Fostering Creativity

To keep my own creativity working over the years, I put together a list of tools and tactics that my customers and I use. Try a few and see if they help you be more creative.

1. Read about different topics at the same time

My favorite gift is a gift certificate to a bookstore. I know I'm not alone in this—reading is addictive. When futurist Alvin Toffler was interviewed on C-Span's *Book TV* about his book *Revolutionary Wealth*, he talked about how he fosters his own creativity.

Like most creative people, he is a voracious reader. But what he emphasized is that, by reading several very different books and articles at the same time, he sees connections that never would have occurred to him if he were not reading these works simultaneously. Information about history, international news stories, and current web trends that shift timeframes, points of view, and location are all included. Learning about all these things at once can make you see a way of combining all sorts of ideas into one effective marketing campaign.

A fun example of this was presented in the movie *Working Girl* released in 1988. A hard working secretary named Tess McGill (Melanie Griffith) tries to get ahead by coming up with a great idea that will get her promoted. Her boss, Katherine Parker (Sigourney Weaver), steals the idea and presents it as her own. To determine who is lying, they ask each person to describe how they arrived at the idea. Tess says she was reading the newspaper and saw the wedding announcement of a TV station owner's daughter. She then read that some radio stations were being sold and put both ideas together. She would help set up the deal for the TV station owner to purchase those radio stations—two separate ideas that came together. Of course her boss Katherine had no answer to the question, and it was obvious she was lying.

2. Try to make things as simple as possible

I'm sure you've noticed that when people want to demonstrate their skill, they present something really complex—lots of PowerPoint slides, not too much clarity. New business ideas should always be considered, but boiling them down to their essence separates the big winners from the also-rans. Take an idea and delete things. See if you can make it stunningly simple.

> ## *CASE STUDY:* Simplicity to greatness
>
> *In the December 2006 issue of Business 2.0, Google founders Sergey Brin and Larry Page talk about how they succeeded with simplicity. They devised a search engine with a home page screen that had merely a search box in which the user typed a keyword. What could be easier? They maintain that that simplicity helped them succeed, and even now, after all their success, they say that simplicity is "an important trend we are focused on."*
>
> *People choose Google because it is easy to use. Can you say the same about your product, service, website? Simplicity can be employed anywhere. Jazz bassist Charles Mingus once said of simplicity, "Making the simple complicated is commonplace; making the complicated simple, awesomely simple, that's creativity."*

3. Bring a sense of design to everything you do

In this century, design matters. It's the language we use to communicate our beliefs and dreams. A well-thought-out website and well-designed web graphics can go a long way toward showing the customer you pay attention to detail.

It doesn't have to be a major investment or initiative, just a little something to show that your company is willing to go the extra mile. Nordstrom instructs their salespeople to come from behind the counter to hand you your purchase. That's how they show their attention to detail and personalize the experience. Think through your sales process and see what you can do at little or no cost to make an impact.

CASE STUDY: Target hits the mark

The people at Target Brands, Inc., are a prime example of how bringing design to the commonplace can succeed. They hired celebrated architect Michael Graves to design a line of household items. These were met with great excitement, and he has created over two hundred items to date. This helped firmly embed their brand idea in your mind—well-designed items at low cost. This thinking helped them leapfrog over the competition.

4. Keep "stages" notebooks

In her book, *The Creative Habit*, Twyla Tharp talks about how Beethoven saved his ideas. He documented everything he created and kept a series of notebooks with an interesting twist—each contained ideas in different stages of development. He had a notebook for early ideas, one for ideas that were in the process of being shaped, and one for final ideas.

He would put a rough idea in the first one and let it incubate. When he came back to the idea, he would pluck it out of that notebook and develop it further in notebook two. Then he would let that idea incubate some more. Each time he went back to an idea, he was able to develop it further with all the knowledge and perspective he had gained since his last look.

Incubate your ideas: This is an invaluable idea for any businessperson who wants to capture and follow ideas from inception to completion. Try a series of stages notebooks and see if that helps you push your ideas along.

5. Keep your focus and keep going

Sometimes when I'm in the middle of a big project, I am reminded of a principle developed by Rosabeth Moss Kanter at the Harvard Business School. In her book, *Confidence: How Winning Streaks and Losing Streaks Begin and End*, she said that when she's working on a project, she always points out to everyone involved that "All projects look like a disaster in the middle." It may not be apparent, but this ties back to creativity in a very direct way. Creativity requires what some people may view as chaos or an inability to control every aspect of the process. When you are in the middle of a project that feels uncontrollable, you need to remember that some of this is required to create a new process.

This is a key notion to keep in mind when you're launching a product or getting your new website up and running. Everyone will remain focused if you prepare them for the ups and downs of completing a project. Winston Churchill echoed a similar sentiment, when he said, "If you are going through Hell, keep going."

6. Collect inspiring quotes and metaphors

Through the years, I have found lots of quotes and thoughts that have inspired me. Anne Miller, author of *Metaphorically Selling*, talks about how she, too, is an inveterate clipper. She keeps personal files of inspiring thoughts and sayings that she can refer to when she wants to give her creativity a boost.

Miller's twist is that she collects clever metaphors along with the quotes from articles, speeches, magazines, movie reviews, etc. These metaphors can be rebent and reshaped to fit her new ideas and products, as well as help her see something in a new and unexpected way.

7. Pay attention to popular culture

This doesn't mean that you have to religiously track who's winning on the TV reality shows (unless you want to). But you should be aware of what your customers are interested in. There are lots of tools that can help you keep abreast of prevailing trends. (I talk about this extensively in Chapter 19.)

The key to making pop culture work for you in a business setting is to continually ask yourself, "What's different today?" What new thing or news story is impacting my customers today? Read everything you can about new ideas and cultural trends. You don't have to try to apply every one of them, but you do need to know what your customer knows. Staying aware of popular culture ensures that you won't suddenly find yourself with an outdated marketing strategy and no customers.

CASE STUDY: Three Questions for Christine Kane, songwriter, performer, and creativity trainer

1. *Do you think that online readers are more interested in creativity now that they have so many great social media tools to express themselves?*

    I think that people who are blogging and discovering social media are finding out how creative they already are, and it surprises them that it's not as big a deal as they thought. It's not creativity with a capital C. Certainly, there are more ways to be out there doing art and being creative, but the model has changed a lot. People are finding that they have to be creative not only in this thing they create but in how they get it out in the world and make it grow.

2. *Why do you think your blog is so well received by such a diverse audience?*

    I see my blog as an extension of my work and music and performances. So, in some ways, my blog audience isn't that much different from my music audience, which has always been somewhat diverse. And, of course, one could argue the many ways that this audience isn't all that diverse when it comes to world view, etc. But what I think attracts readers to me or to any blogger is voice and authenticity. I'm blogging about living in the world successfully as a creative person.

This is what I do in my day-to-day life. And I screw up quite a bit. If there's one gift that blogging gives people, it's that things get demystified. And I work at making the creative and business life of an artist a little less holier-than-thou. I think people like to know that I'm a lot like them.

3. *What's your best tip for someone who wants to apply creativity to their work?*

Silence and space. I do corporate creativity training, and I teach creativity to government leaders. (These are among the many great things that have come out of starting a blog!) The most common block to creativity I see in the workplace is that people's lives are too crammed full of stuff, from clutter to background televisions to busyness. New ideas don't have a chance to enter if the space is already full. I encourage people to go through the intense discomfort of quiet—even if it's as simple as turning off the music on their commute. Of course, that's just a starting place. But it's a big one.

For additional information, check out Christine's blog at www.christinekane.com/blog

Mind Mapping

Many small business owners lurch from fad to fad with their website and online marketing, only to be disappointed when they fail. Just because the Web moves and changes much more quickly than traditional media does not mean you can succeed without the planning and testing needed to build any business.

Mind Mapping can help you get through the planning process with a lot less pain. Mind Mapping has been called the "Swiss Army knife of the brain." It helps organize and clarify your ideas and takes your thinking to the next level. It works like your brain does, so it's easy to pick up and use immediately.

Figure 3.1

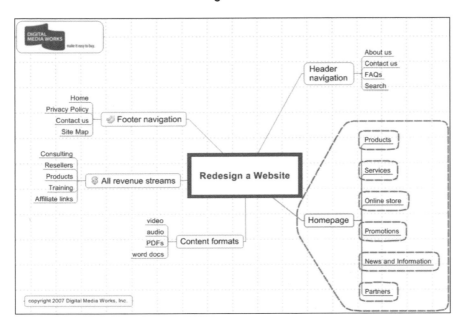

You can map out your thoughts with something as simple as colored pencils and a piece of paper, or you can upgrade to some of the great software that's now available. One terrific thing about using mapping software over paper and pencils is the ability to move things around and delete them easily.

I use MindManager from Mindjet. The maps you see in this book are created using MindManager Pro 7. It is integrated with MS Office and other software programs so you can put it into spreadsheets and text documents, etc. You can download a free trial at www.mindjet.com/us/download/. They also have lots of good examples and information about how to use maps. One of the more important features of MindManager is that it lets you create notes right in the map and hyperlinks to documents, websites, and spreadsheets. It's also integrated with some third-party project software, so that you can track work plans. I've created several custom "dashboard" maps for my clients so they can accomplish many marketing tasks from one map.

I use Mind Maps to develop Internet strategies and campaigns for all my online business clients. I have used this tool for many years and highly recommend it—it will change the way you develop your thoughts and plans. It helps you literally see what you're thinking.

When businesspeople feel confused and isolated, they can turn to a Mind Map to clarify they're thinking. The map often provides visual evidence that an idea is right for them—regardless of what others say.

It also is a great help when you are overwhelmed—it provides an easy way to get the task started. Revamping your website can seem daunting, but using a mapping process helps you put your big picture together in small chunks so that the task doesn't seem insurmountable. Whenever I see people struggling with or avoiding projects, I suggest they start with a map.

QUICK Tip

The original: Tony Buzan developed Mind Mapping in the UK in the late 1960s, to help students learn and solve problems more effectively. This technique has grown worldwide and continues to make use of exciting new things we learn about the brain. To learn more about Buzan and his work, you can check out his *The Mind Map Book*, and online at www.BuzanWorld.com.

Benefits of Mind Mapping for Web marketers

1. You can view the "big picture" and the details at the same time.

When you look at a completed Mind Map, you and your staff can see the "big picture" and all the details that create it at the same time. This helps managers focus on the overall strategy while those tasked with the details can focus on their part, and everyone can see their contribution to the whole. Looking at your "business" on a map that shows you the whole picture can be an enlightening experience. You get to see what you create from start to finish, and you'll also be able to see if you are on the wrong track.

2. It encourages creative input.

Creating a map stimulates creativity by using pictures and colors and lines of different widths and spaces. You will see connections and associations you never thought of before. Also, everyone who looks at it might have a different way of seeing it—this could be a great way to have all your employees participate in the big picture and find some great ideas.

3. It's not linear, so you don't have to move things around to make new ideas fit.

You can put ideas on the map as they occur to you, wherever they seem to fit best. In a standard outline format you need to create a hierarchy, but with a Mind Map you are able to make a natural association and develop a step-by-step plan for accomplishing the goal later.

4. It helps you create new products and content more easily.

If you want to brainstorm new product ideas, you can easily put the main ideas on a map and quickly generate lots of new thoughts. Once the ideas are placed on the map, you'll be able to see how they can be worked into products. A good illustration of this is a monthly company newsletter; you can create one map that you use as a template for the newsletter, and then easily see how to create twelve for the year.

5. It lets you see what you forgot before you launch.

Mind Maps highlight omissions. When you follow the same process and the same lists all the time, you forget or just don't see what's missing. Looking at the material in a new way helps you analyze it and spot any holes.

Mind Maps also work well in meetings where the participants have diverse skills. Rather than focus on their specific skills, you focus on ideas. Engineers don't need to supply engineering ideas, just good ideas. The marketing group has their way of looking at things, the developers theirs, and management still another. When people feel that others are receptive to their ideas, they are more likely to look for solutions. This is exactly the kind of atmosphere you want to create when you meet to solve business problems.

When you complete a Mind Mapping session you can have:

- A working map that helps you find new revenue streams: a look at all your revenue streams on one sheet of paper will help you brainstorm what's missing.
- A clear understanding of resources needed to complete tasks: you can see the scope of your task and determine the amount of time and materials.
- A complete look at ongoing budget needs: when you see the project as a whole you can determine how much maintenance costs will be.
- A strong website that meets your goals and generates revenue: no more guessing and hit or miss pages being created. You'll know how every page fits into your plan.

Once you have the "big picture" mapped out, you can focus on drilling-down through the sections. Often you will see new ideas jump out at you when you look at your business in this new way. Mind Maps make it easy to analyze where you are now. That's why I use them to develop new websites or redesign current ones.

CASE STUDY: Using Mind Mapping

To understand how to apply this to your business, let me detail the process we used with a client of Digital Media Works. A small high-tech client called us in to analyze their website. They wanted to make it easier for their customers to find information and buy products. We called for a mapping session that included "major stakeholders." Since they were a small company, this included people from third-party groups as well as a webmaster, a VP, and a Sales Director. Mind Mapping works with groups of any size. If you are the principal of a small business, creating a map of your company is an important first step in getting your arms around potential revenue streams.

After a brief presentation of the Mind Mapping process, we began by looking at the websites of two of their strongest competitors. To jump-start the effort, I created two Mind Maps before the session, one for each of the competitors. This helped everyone see how the process worked and got them thinking about how they compared to their competition.

We looked at the completed maps labeled "Competitor 1" and "Competitor 2." We left off identifying names because we wanted to have an objective look at the maps. These were only "top line" maps with major home page branches. We focused strictly on the essentials—the information their competitor's visitors see first. We didn't compare "look and feel" or complexity of back-end systems. This helped to crystallize what their competitors thought was most important—companies put the most important company information on their home pages, so in this way we were able to determine what they chose to provide their customers with. This was an enlightening experience.

Next we mapped our client's website. Due to the earlier mapping, they were already thinking about what their competitors were doing and how they could do it better. The map quickly grew and evolved. We knew that their competitors were providing a variety of information formats, so they decided to beef up their information area. To improve their conversion rates, they decided to construct an easier path to buying a product. We spent the next two hours developing a very strong website structure.

Next, we allowed the map to incubate overnight. Everyone was eager to keep going, but physically tired. This was a good time to stop. I recommend no more than two hours for the first session. An incubation period is key. During the incubation period, I revised the map to make sure everything was captured and asked team members to review it to make sure all the ideas we generated were there. After an incubation period, you see the map more clearly and you are able to brainstorm with a fresh eye.

We began the next session two days later and the map continued to evolve until it contained solutions to all the issues they could think of. My design/development team then took the map and started to focus on the information they needed to develop work plans. Now that they grasped the big picture goals and the details, they could efficiently plan for resource *usage, budgets, design, etc. This is key because it saves time and money—you don't have big revelations after development has begun.*

We proceeded to review and complete the steps until the new website was up and running. Our client quickly experienced a 50 percent increase in sales revenue over their previous design, and the benefits continue to accrue.

Try this technique on your website—you can do it yourself or ask other stakeholders to participate. I'm sure it will help you see your site and any other projects you need to plan in a whole new way.

CASE STUDY: Three Questions for Chuck Frey, founder of www.innovationtools.com and author of http://mindmapping. typepad.com/

1. *Chuck, how are small business owners using Mind Mapping to their advantage?*

   Small business owners are the people most likely to purchase Mind Mapping software, because they're always on the lookout for tools that give them better insights and ideas, and visual mapping is great for that. They're using it to do things like capture and organize ideas, write business plans, manage projects, and collaborate efficiently.

2. *How are you using Mind Mapping software to streamline your work?*

   Here's the best example I have: each month, I write an e-newsletter that contains between twenty and thirty short, one-paragraph articles. The content is contained in a variety of forms, including email messages,

Word documents, and web pages. I use MindManager to keep track of all of those materials, using its advanced linking capabilities. When it comes time to write the e-newsletter, I just follow those links to gather all of the raw materials for that issue. It saves me many hours of time.

3. *Have social media tools helped foster innovation? How?*

   Yes. Here's an example: getting customers more involved in your product development efforts is an area where social media tools can be an enabler. By using this technology to invite customers into online conversations on an ongoing basis, you can get a better idea of what their real "pain points" are. And that can lead you to insights about their needs.

Additional Resources: Chuck Frey's Power Tips & Strategies for Mind Mapping Software, http://www.mindmap-ebook.com/v2/

Chapter

Think Like a Direct Response Copywriter

There are some that only employ words for the purpose of disguising their thoughts.

—*Voltaire*

If you're just getting started marketing online today you're lucky. You don't have to break old habits and overcome the notion that you can control the customer message. Longtime marketers are struggling with that new reality every day. With the customer in control, everything is turned on its head—marketers can't dictate how customers will perceive their brand.

Given this climate of change and the new emphasis on social media, we might be tempted to throw out all the tried-and-true methods of marketing and selling. This would be a big mistake. Certain things about how people buy will always be true, and certain methods you use to convince them to buy will always work. One of these is direct response marketing. Direct response marketing is marketing that requires a prospect to take action and directly respond to your promotion. A solicitation in the mail for a magazine subscription is a common example. When a prospect responds to your promotion, she has qualified herself. A key weapon in your arsenal is to think like a direct response copywriter. These skills apply to selling online more than selling in almost any other medium. If you learn about how to apply direct response principles, you will be well-equipped to create online campaigns.

There's nothing revolutionary about direct mail principles—they work. They've worked for one hundred years and will probably work for one hundred more. What is new is that applying these principles to online marketing works remarkably well. If you read an old textbook on direct mail marketing, you'll find the rules apply to your brand-new website. The vehicle for bringing offers to customers has simply moved online. So, let's see what we need to borrow from the world of direct response advertising to be successful.

Direct Response Rules—AIDA

The acronym AIDA has been used by direct response copywriters to help them focus on the key actions they want their customers to take—Attention, Interest, Desire, and Action.

Look for the linear: Even though this formula works, it can be a bit more difficult to make it happen online. That's because online text is not linear. You can't count on the reader seeing everything in the exact order you want. People jump from link to link to follow a trail that suits their needs. However, there are ways to assist users in their trip through your site. Let's take the direct response AIDA acronym apart and see how it applies to your website.

Attention: Headlines Are Important

To grab attention, headlines are critically important. The commonly quoted statistic is that eight out of ten people will read the headline, but only two out of ten will read more than that—so you can see that getting the headline right is critical. Also, it's been found that most people only scan online content, not read it. This is important—it means you've got three seconds to grab their attention and make them read further.

Scanning mishaps: Recently, I created a blog post with the headline "Are you niche enough?" A reader wrote back, "I quickly scanned the headline and thought it read: 'Are you nice enough?'" The good news was, he went back and read it again just to make sure—it got his attention. That was the goal—to make him stop and pay attention.

When creating headlines there are several styles to consider. They are:

1. Question-based—Ask people something you know they want the answer to: Who wants to earn more and work less?

2. Problem-based—Figure out what crucial business problem your product can solve: Is your marketing strategy missing a vital link?
3. Curiosity factor—Use a term people might not know, but that they can see the importance of: Are your products lacking the wow factor?
4. How to—Tell them how to do something you know they want to do: How to reduce your weight without exercise
5. Testimonials—Have other people tell your audience how amazing your products and services are: Jane Jones is a miracle worker. We made a $100,000 extra in one week following her advice.

QUICK Tip

Good headlines get the reader to move from the subject to the content of your promotion. You need to make them entertaining and easy to understand at a glance. Your headlines need to be catchy and suggest that if they read further, they will be rewarded.

Most copywriters say that writing headlines is easy to learn. You need to know what works and what doesn't. So let's look at some of the key things you need to know about writing headlines for the Web:

- Headlines must promise something to the reader. The promise should be fulfilled later in the copy.
- When you are writing headlines, be aware of your keywords. Search engines will find you more easily if you are able to include your keyword and get your reader's attention at the same time. The key is to do this without sacrificing a powerful headline.
- Great headlines don't need to be created from scratch. Copywriters use what they call a "swipe file." A swipe file is just what it sounds like. It's a file of tried-and-true headlines that have worked for other copywriters forever. Experts have used them successfully by varying the headline to suit the offer. The key to doing this correctly is understanding why the headline worked, and then applying it to your offer.

For example, take the headline, "Who else wants to _____?" This headline has been used by copywriters for ads, articles, and now blog posts and online sales letters. If you search Google for that headline you'll get almost half a million references. The promise of this headline is that you are identifying yourself as someone who wants what the headline promises, such as:

- Who else wants to <u>save money</u>?
- Who else wants to <u>know how to choose a daycare</u>?
- Who else wants to <u>know how to spot a gifted or talented kid</u>?
- Who else wants to <u>save on watering bills</u>?

QUICK Tip

John Caples, considered the father of advertising testing, created the now famous headline, "They Laughed When I Sat Down at the Piano, But When I Started to Play!" It's in every copywriter's swipe file. His life spanned the entire twentieth century and he greatly influenced the field of advertising. He believed that effective headlines should "get to the point quickly." There's no magic to it. You just need to be aware of the underlying principles.

Alert!

Your swipe file: Consider building your own swipe file. When you are struggling to write online copy, it will give you ideas and help propel you forward. You can find material in magazines, newspapers, brochures, junk mail, sales letters, and the like.

If you find these ideas online you can print them out and put them in a folder, or you can use a free online program like i-Lighter. i-Lighter is like a yellow highlighter pen for the Web. It lets you highlight and clip items and store them in digital folders. To check out the program you can go to www.ilighter.com.

The "So" Question

When you are writing sales copy here's a trick to help you uncover your message: the "SO?" question. To get your reader's attention you want to put the benefits of your product or service right in the headline. My clients often have long lists of features that they want to present to the customer. To help focus the list, concentrate on the benefits of those features.

Look at these features and ask the SO? Question:

Before: "Our software has built-in upgrades."
After: "Our software has built-in upgrades **SO?—you never have to buy another copy of the product, saving you time and money.**"
Before: "Our plant food contains three special growth minerals."
After: "Our plant food contains three special growth minerals **SO?— your plants grow to twice the size with half the work!**"

You get the idea. You need to use the feature as the jumping-off point for the benefit. If you make a list of features and then compare it to a list of resulting benefits, you will see why you need to do this for all your copy. It's a compelling reason to buy, and it works. This applies to software, hardware, garden ornaments, CDs, insurance, or anything else you sell.

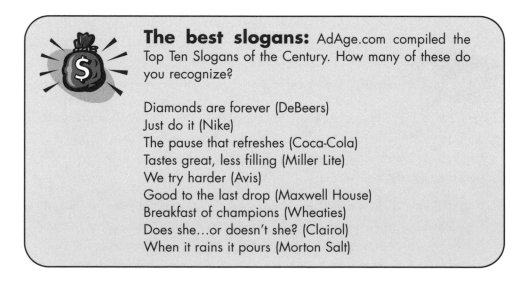

The best slogans: AdAge.com compiled the Top Ten Slogans of the Century. How many of these do you recognize?

Diamonds are forever (DeBeers)
Just do it (Nike)
The pause that refreshes (Coca-Cola)
Tastes great, less filling (Miller Lite)
We try harder (Avis)
Good to the last drop (Maxwell House)
Breakfast of champions (Wheaties)
Does she...or doesn't she? (Clairol)
When it rains it pours (Morton Salt)

Interest: Is that a Fact?

Once you craft a great headline, you've gotten someone's attention. Next, you need to create a real interest in your product. The best way to do this is with facts, stories, anecdotes, anything that causes the reader to relate to the content in some way. You want the reader to be able to immediately spot everyone's favorite acronym—WIIFM (what's in it for me?) This means that the copy should focus on what interests her—not what interests your company. Don't tell her how about your company is the first to create a comb with rubber tips—tell her how the comb will benefit her hairstyle. There is a place for a story about how you invented the comb, but it's not in your sales copy.

Alert!

Be a consumer: Be aware of ads that spend too much time talking about the company and not enough focusing on customer benefits. Once you go looking for them, you'll see they exist everywhere. Most often they are written by in-house marketers who put their boss's approval over getting the sale.

QUICK Tip

Search smarter: Copernic Agent Basic is a very useful piece of software for performing specialized searches online. It allows you to search over one thousand search engines simultaneously, performing what is referred to as a "super search" of the Web. It will help you find lots of useful anecdotes and information to spice up your copy.

Copernic Agent Basic has created ten different categories and selected the best search engines for each, which helps you find exactly what you're looking for. It also removes duplicates, which is a real time-saver. There's a free version of the software at http://www.copernic.com/en/products/agent/download .html. They also have two advanced versions that are inexpensive and have more features.

Desire: Power Words

Next we turn to power words. Power words are the key words you need to use to create desire for your product in the consumer. And there are words that still have the power to make sophisticated online customers buy. Regardless of the time and place, there are certain words that always generate excitement or convey a mood.

Every time you watch a movie or a YouTube video, you are affected by the language and the message it conveys. Start paying attention to what captures your attention the most, and don't forget it when you create content for your website. If you're selling flashlights you can say, "Our flashlight is very powerful" or you can say "The power of our flashlight will knock you off your feet!" Help the reader to visualize the power of your product.

QUICK Tip

Careful with the exclamations: What has changed in copywriting as online customers become more sophisticated is the tendency to scorn hyperbole. If everything is fantastic! wonderful! magnificent!, then nothing stands out. It all seems the same, and it seems like a lie. Authenticity is a hallmark of social media and should guide whatever you write.

An honest assessment and presentation of your product doesn't need to be boring to be truthful. As Seth Godin wrote in his book, *All Marketers are Liars*, "You don't get to just sit down and make up a story and expect that people will believe it merely because you want them to." Find an entertaining way to tell the truth. (See more about this in Step 3, Story.)

QUICK Tip

If you want to join an online community of people interested in finding and sharing a wealth of Web information using advanced search tools, check out Derek Franklin's online community at www.topicseekers.com

 There are a number of great books you can use to assist you in selecting the right power words. Two examples are *More Words that Sell* by Richard Bayan and *Phrases that Sell* by Edward Werz and Sally Germain. These are collections of words that help you convey your message by matching words to feelings. For example, to evoke the idea of laughter, you can use a word like "giggle," or for enthusiasm the word "zest." This will make it easier for you to craft just the right sales copy.

You may also want to consider a professional copywriter for your main product descriptions. It's worth considering if you know your skills are limited in that area. Your visitor won't buy from a poorly written website, no matter how good your product is. He won't get to that point. He'll be stuck back at "Attention" and never get to "Desire" or "Action."

You can check www.elance.com or search online for freelance copywriters. The key is to make sure you carefully explain exactly what your goal is for the project and what you expect to receive when it's completed. Make sure to agree upon a price up-front so there are no surprises. You can't underestimate the value of good copywriting.

Action: Craft Your Information Path

So now it's time to get your customers to take action. What makes online selling seem so mysterious? Why does one person buy quickly and another procrastinate? One reason is that people have different buying styles. In order to accommodate your customers, you need to account for all types when you craft an offer. Carefully tailor your message so that it appeals to each audience.

Let's look at four audience types and see what kind of content is needed for each.

1. The "trendsetter"
   Often called the early adopter, this person wants the newest and the latest and won't hesitate to experiment. For them, part of the fun of buying is taking the risk that the product might not live up to its hype. What they need is clearly defined prices and terms and a quick checkout.

QUICK Tip

Online areas to target:

Have a clear, well-run shopping cart in place. Make it easy for her to buy quickly and leave satisfied. Make sure you send an email confirmation that makes it clear that a product was purchased and a credit card or other payment process was used.

2. The "hands-on tester"
   This type is straightforward. He wants to get the product in his hands and toy with it to satisfy himself that it works and he likes it. If you sell services, you can offer a free "one-time" offer or consultation. With products, it can be a bit trickier. Watch out for people who love to test and return. The majority of buyers are honest, but there are a few who have no intention of keeping the product.

QUICK Tip

Online areas to target:

If you're selling software, create a trial version of the product or develop a sample. You can also offer a thirty- or sixty-day guaranteed return. I recommend a sixty-day return phase—the longer someone waits to return something the likelier they are to forget about it. This doesn't produce a raving fan, but at least you got someone to try your product. If you're lucky, they might pass it on to a friend or family member who likes it.

3. The "fact checker"
   This is a cautious person, who likes all his ducks in a row before making a decision. He won't buy until all his questions are answered. Your job is to make sure he has everything he needs from you to make that decision. This is the type of person who benefits the most from online shopping—he can surf, compare, and read product reviews until he's satisfied.

QUICK Tip

Online areas to target:

Make sure your website and other venues include multiple information formats, audio, video, white papers that detail a successful case study, etc. Have plenty of downloadable PDFs, articles, photos of the product, etc. Consider conducting teleseminars and webinars where people can ask questions.

4. The "hasty buyer"
    This is the impulse-buyer, who develops buyer's remorse right after purchasing. This usually is not a reflection on your product or service—it's just his habit. Knowing that this buyer exists, you can be ready and help him get over his initial reaction. You want to send him tutorials or other things that will get him started using the product as soon as possible.

QUICK Tip

Online areas to target:

Make it clear to this buyer that your service does not end with the sale. Sending thank you emails and newsletters, offering online help and tutorials, and hosting an online community all show him that you stand behind your product and make him feel good about his purchase.

Launching a New Product

So how can you put all this together to bring your product—and its marketing campaign—into the world? Throughout the life of your business, you will be introducing new products or services on a regular basis. Think about how you can structure these launches and marketing materials to focus on the total customer experience. This means looking at the process of buying from start to finish.

If the goal is to get an email address, start from the very beginning and make sure that you have a process that gets the customer there efficiently and easily. If the goal is to get the customer to request a free sample, analyze that from start to finish and be sure that the process has clearly defined steps to make that happen. Then look at how you can encourage the next sale. Determine how the customer will see your initial information through to the final purchase, and make sure you're fulfilling the goals you've set for yourself and that the customer is satisfied.

Five things you must do before you launch

1. Make sure your marketing message is ready.

You are eager to get the product out there, but if your message isn't clear, your customers won't buy. Ask yourself whether your headlines support the product's main benefits. Does your new product make the process faster or easier? Does it help simplify a complex process? What are you really offering your customer that they don't have now? If you don't present the message clearly, they won't search for it and you've missed an opportunity.

2. Check your shopping cart.

Having a quick, simple way for customers to select and pay for your merchandise sounds simple, but it's probably the single biggest reason products fail. Some shopping carts are hard, sometimes impossible to buy from—which makes purchasing your product hard if not impossible. Make it easy! Not only do you need to make sure the cart process is simple to understand, make sure it WORKS. This needs to be perfect before you launch.

3. Plan your advertising and PR.

This one can be very challenging. You need to have all your marketing and PR basics in place before you start selling. Are you buying an ad in a newsletter? Are you writing an article to submit to websites? It's okay to start small if your budget is limited, but you have to get the word out about your product and build buzz before you launch.

4. Explain to your employees what you are selling.

This sounds obvious, but don't assume they will know what you have in mind for the product unless you tell them. They are ambassadors to your customers. If they don't understand the marketing pitch, they can't explain it. Don't assume they'll read the materials you created—meet with them and discuss it.

5. Send discounts to current customers.

Did you forget your current customers? They need to receive special treatment. They are predisposed to buying from you and could provide good word-of-mouth. This entitles them to a discount or special offer. Send them an email or special newsletter with the offer. Make sure you track the results so see how well your message worked with your current customers.

In summary, the key to thinking like a copywriter requires that you present your marketing message as the answer to a problem your customer is seeking. Assume that it has value and that it will make her life easier, more productive, more fun, etc. If you don't believe your product has value, you won't be able to sustain the message.

Let's review the "must do's" for effective online copywriting:

• Create an experience.

You will not be present when your customer "visits" your store. You need to rely on your words and graphics to set a mood and prepare your customer for a positive experience. Take care to make your landing page, home page, or other online venue communicate that you value your customer. Your customer won't buy if they are annoyed by your lack of attention to important details like navigation and shopping cart.

• Carefully choose the word to fit the mood.

Use the books I recommend along with many others that offer the right word to suit the need. Word choice is very important. Don't settle on the first word that pops into your mind.

• Provide headlines that offer an answer.

Copywriters spend hours writing and rewriting headlines. They can literally work on one hundred variations of a headline until they think it's right. Don't feel you are wasting time if you spend some time crafting a headline that will really get your customer's attention.

• Emphasize the benefits that come from buying.

When you write about your products, make sure you lead with the benefits and not the features. You will entice your visitor to read further.

• Give interesting examples of others who have benefited from buying.

People need to be reassured that others have purchased and been satisfied with your product or service. Make sure they have no doubt.

Okay, now you know the reason why you need to think like a direct response copywriter. In the next chapter we look at how your can reach success by thinking like a publisher.

Chapter

You're a Publisher Now!

The skill of writing is to create a context in which other people can think.

—Edwin Schlossberg

- ▶ **How to Think Like a Publisher**
- ▶ **RSS**
- ▶ **Permission-Based Emails**
- ▶ **Widgets**
- ▶ **Webinars and Teleseminars**
- ▶ **E-books**
- ▶ **You Need a Mailing List**
- ▶ **Email Software**

Every online marketer has to think like a publisher, because you are one—you are the publisher of information in a variety of formats that will persuade customers to buy your products and champion them to others. If you do it right, you can create a life-long customer.

Defining your niche audiences and analyzing your website content are critically important actions that ensure your "publishing empire" suits your audience's special needs. You'll need to provide content that is totally unexpected and stands out from the online clutter.

How to Think Like a Publisher

In an online environment, QVC.com is as much a publisher as Sourcebooks, Inc. The content and format of their products are different, but the marketing copy they create helps influence the customer's decision to buy.

QVC.com includes videos of people discussing the benefits of their products and features customer ratings. Sourcebooks.com has their www.Austenfans.com site that brings Jane Austen fans together to celebrate her legacy and discuss books written in her style. One has videos and customer ratings, the other has discussions and author interviews, and these fit the needs and preferences of their audiences. QVC.com shoppers are likely very visually oriented, as it's a television program—so videos will appeal strongly to them. Jane Austen fans are likely readers who enjoy talking about books, so text and discussion work well for that website.

Once you think like a publisher who tailors her products and marketing efforts to her specific audience, you will be able to create the materials you need to connect with your customers. So how do you get started thinking like a publisher?

The Benefits of Thinking Like a Publisher

1. It focuses your attention on the big picture and helps you create your content strategy.

Having a content strategy is key: you need to look at all your content as a library of items that can be plucked off the shelf when the appropriate message and format is needed. Businesses usually create content on the fly. This is inefficient and creates a slapdash collection of materials.

For example, a white paper is written when it's needed for a business proposal, or a podcast is recorded when you run out of ideas for blog posts. This is a "hit or miss" way to approach content creation. If you think about all the types of content you'll need when you create your website (or when you give it a good overhaul) you'll have pieces that fit together and build synergy. Then as you add new items, you'll know how they fit in your strategy.

QUICK Tip

Content control: Create one main folder on your server called "Information" which includes subfolders with all the categories of marketing content—newsletter archives, videos, webinars, press releases, case studies, white papers, etc. If you have a large library, subdivide them by product. This way you can have everything in one place for you or your staff to turn to. It's very easy to lose or misplace items or forget you have them, and then their value is lost to you. This makes creating consistent sales copy easy.

2. It helps you think about encouraging repeat customers.

When you look at what people will read and hear when they see your brand, you'll be able to think about how you can encourage them to return for more. People go online to explore and learn something, entertain themselves, find a specific product or service, and connect with others. When you are creating content, you need to define the purpose. For example, some content on your website should be there to educate and entertain your customer so that they will return often. By visiting your site frequently, customers will view you as a trusted information source and have the opportunity to see your current offers. MarthaStewart.com has employed this idea by creating educational content on a variety of subjects and then repurposing the content for the web, radio, magazines, video, and television. If you are interested in one of the topics covered, you will return often to find updated content in different formats.

3. It makes you aware that you can create great content whenever you prepare a presentation.

Thinking like a publisher means finding the content that your audience wants and presenting it in the right medium. If you are having a day-long conference, you can record video interviews of the presenters to put online. If you are meeting with a consumer group, you can ask each one to record a thought about why they use your product and use them as video testimonials. The understanding that you need to constantly create new content like any good publisher helps you find new opportunities.

Now let's turn to the tools available to you that for your content online quickly and easily. Bear in mind that these technologies did not exist even a decade ago. Their introduction revolutionized the way we communicate—putting a printing press in everyone's hands.

RSS

RSS is a very important tool for the online publisher. RSS stands for "Really Simple Syndication" and luckily, it's easier to use than it is to explain. RSS was developed in 1999 by Netscape to distribute information. In a nutshell, this tool takes digital information and puts it into a readable format that can be sent to those who request it online. This formatted data is called a feed and you create it by "burning a feed."

You can burn a feed for your blog, your newsletter, or any content you think readers will find interesting. Once you have a feed, readers can subscribe and receive the feed each time it is updated, as an email or in your feed reader (see below). Probably the most well-known feed creator is www.feedburner.com, which was acquired by Google in 2007. Two others are www.feedblitz.com and www.feedforall.com.

RSS is viewed as one of the most important Web 2.0 tools available, because it can be useful to you for both distributing your own information and collecting information that you need to run your business. Let's look at both sides of that coin.

Benefits of RSS Feeds

• It's chosen by you, for you.

RSS feeds are information that you requested—you're not being bombarded by unwanted ads or information you can't use. It's a great way to organize information and track trend information. You can learn what's new with your favorite team or track financial data, and the information comes *to you*.

• You can remain anonymous.

You don't have to reveal your email address; you can have the information sent to a feed reader, which doesn't run the risk of generating more spam.

• It saves you time.

You don't have to take any action to receive it; it comes to you whenever it is updated.

• It's in whatever format you prefer.

You can receive information in whatever format suits you—audio, video, text, etc.

RSS also benefits you as a marketer in two important ways: It helps you get your product information to the right audience of potential buyers, and it helps you get more traffic and visibility for your brand. Also, RSS information is highly "prized" by search engines because it's targeted and constantly updated. This boost in the search engine rankings will help your customers find you more easily.

QUICK Tip

Keep your customers informed: here are some ways you can use RSS to keep your customers updated:

- New product announcements
- Promotions and discounts

- Podcast and video interviews
- Recall information
- Product tips and hints
- Vendor and supplier notices
- News releases

Content Aggregators (Feed Readers)

You may be wondering what the term "content aggregator" means. It's a complex sounding name for the tool that allows you to bring all your feeds together in one place—basically, it's a personalized home page. You choose what you want to know and the way you want to consume it. This means that you can have all your feeds—email accounts, blogs, social networks, instant message, photos, videos, podcasts and widgets, sent to one online place to view.

Or if you prefer, you can have one just for blogs, one for podcasts, etc. Most feed readers are free and there are many. Some commonly used ones are iGoogle and My Yahoo. I use Netvibes because it is set up to easily hold all kinds of content in one place. It can be found at www.netvibes.com. Whatever feed reader you choose, just go to the site and you'll get directions on how to set it up and add anything you'd like to access.

Set up a personal feed reader to start building your repository of interesting content. Whenever you see some interesting information like a blog or news feed, arrange to have it sent to you and housed in one place. (For more specific details, see Chapter 19: Tracking Your Success.)

Permission-Based Emails

If you think email marketing is losing steam, think again. A March 2007 Forrester report on email marketing shows that people who buy from email links and ads spend 138 percent more than those who do not. Email click-through rates (CTRs) have not changed since 2003. That's a good reason to continue to use emails to promote your business. First let's look at the terms used in email marketing to invite people to join your mailing list. You can have an "opt in" list. Opt in means that people have to take action to **sign up** to your list. An "opt out" list means that they have to take action to **get off** your list. In other words, with an opt out list, YOU sign someone up and they have to remove themselves. Be warned: opt out emails can be considered spam depending on how someone got on your list.

Avoid spam: Spam is an unsolicited email sent in bulk. Most people consider a list they did not sign up for to be spam. Others argue that if you have a prior business relationship with someone you can send them an email. Spam is a great concern to anyone with an email address, and you avoid it in your marketing efforts.

If someone wants your information and subscribes to a list, they'll be much more responsive. An important thing to remember is that it's not that you want to sign up tons of people to your list; you want to sign up potential buyers to your list. People who are interested in your company enough to sign up for email alerts will likely buy your product; people who get your emails by surprise will just be irritated.

Be diligent: How can you avoid sending spam? Be diligent about following the rules. Make sure to check current spam compliance policies. As of this writing, when you send subscriber emails in the form of newsletters and broadcast emails you need to:

1. Have a physical mailing address on your email
2. Have a posted privacy policy
3. Have a way for subscribers to opt out.

Also, you are banned from using false or misleading header information and prohibited from using deceptive subject lines. Obviously, common sense dictates that you don't want to sell the names on your list or violate the trust they gave you when they provided you with their email address.

Once you create the content for your email you'll want to test whether your message will pass through the spam filter. A good free tool is Spam Assassin (http://spamasa ssin.apache.org/). Certain words trigger a spam ranking (like "Free," "Offer," and "Cheap"), and these tools help ensure that your email is not tagged as spam.

Widgets

Widgets are a hot topic—they enhance your ability to publish targeted information. A widget is a small application that you can insert in your blog, website, or other online page to provide information. For example, you've seen the Yahoo weather report widget that allows you to keep updated about the latest weather conditions on your home page. Yahoo has hundreds of widgets (check here to see examples: http://widgets.yahoo.com/), as do Google (http://desktop.google.com/plugins/) and Facebook, among others.

But widgets are much more than just the next bright shiny web toy. They let you build and control your own little information worlds—you can be a content programmer. You decide where each widget is placed so that you can create a completely custom environment. If you want to keep updated on your favorite TV shows, you can get a widget that will let you know when the next episode will be on. You can find widgets for everything from baseball and basketball news to best-selling children's books. The list is endless.

A widget is:

- Easy to put anywhere
- A big aid in viral marketing
- Used by marketers and their clients
- Able to send a variety of content in many different formats, e.g. video, audio, pictures

Using widgets for marketing: As a marketer, widgets hold great promise. They allow the customer to place your company videos, pictures, and more where they want them to keep updated on your offers. They package information and provide it to an interested reader. Even more exciting is that they provide a new avenue for getting information out to your customers and experimenting with new content ideas.

Netscape founder Marc Andreessen is quoted in *Businessweek* as saying, "I think the Internet is going through a major, major shift. Concepts are now able to spread on a million Web sites. It's super exciting because you can get huge scale very quickly. The big widgets have the potential to become the new networks." Social networking site Facebook was shocked by the huge response when they opened their service to allow widgets, and there is lots more to come.

Amazon has developed some widgets that make it easier for members of their affiliate program, "Amazon Associates," to sell their products. As an associate I can now put these widgets on my blog, website, and social network and recommend books and other products appropriate for my audience. Widgets are the classic answer to my ongoing call to "make it easy to buy."

On my blog (http://www.marketingmessageblog.com) I have a variety of widgets that provide my readers with additional content that they would find useful. For example, I use a Smart Links widget from Adaptive Blue.com that allows me to recommend books and provide readers with additional information about books I recommend, without my having to create the content. I also have a Squidoo lensroll widget that allows me to link directly to my Squidoo.com lenses (see page 188 for more info on Squidoo). In each case the widget was created by a content provider who wanted to make it easy for me to share their information with my customers.

Webinars and Teleseminars

Real-time online meetings in the form of webinars and teleseminars are great ways for companies to share information with clients or with virtual offices or employees. As the tools get less expensive and the technology improves, more and more businesses are taking advantage of them. A teleseminar allows you to set up a meeting time for interested users to call in via phone and listen to you interview someone, provide information, or take questions in real-time. A webinar takes this one step further by allowing users to log onto a service that hosts a visual meeting along with the audio. Everyone can see the same screen and a presentation is conducted there, also in real-time. Webinar companies like GoToMeeting.com and WebEx.com provide the ability to make a detailed sales call without the expense and hassle of travel. It's a great way to share the screen and collaborate on projects, as well as help enhance productivity and make it easier to meet deadlines.

Try teleseminars: Many BtoB companies dismiss the idea of using teleseminars as lead generators—they seem to only use webinars. I think this is a mistake. Teleseminars are inexpensive to conduct and there are several companies that provide free conference calling services. FreeConferenceCall.com and FreeConference .com are two examples. You can have a teleseminar about a new product release and interview a leading guru on the subject. You can then put the teleseminar on your blog and newsletter. Think about using both tactics as lead generators.

E-books

In 2006, the Association of American Publishers and the International Digital Publishing Forum reported that the sales of e-books generated $20 million in revenue. E-books are gaining favor among Internet readers. This news should encourage you to create e-books for your customers. The digital book format is typically a multi-page PDF file that can easily be downloaded. This format is exploding and people find it increasingly easy to find and read information this way. With the advent of digital book readers, like the e-book reader Kindle from Amazon, this market will surely grow.

To find topics for e-books you should look at the benefits people derive from using your products. For example, for a custom electronics store you could have "surround sound makes movies come to life." This could lead to an e-book about "How to maximize the use of surround sound in your media room." For a business that sells pet supplies you could have an e-book on "How to keep your pet safe when you travel." The key to these e-books is that **you** are providing custom information for your customers. You want them to view your website as a place to find top-flight information on their topic of interest. Think about e-books as you would any other marketing piece that can educate your customer and generate leads. Don't be thrown by the word "book." It doesn't have to have hundreds of pages to be considered an e-book. If you are concerned that your content is too short to be called an e-book, call it a "special report."

I am not specifically suggesting that you sell them, (although if you have an e-book that customers will pay for, by all means, sell it). I **am** suggesting that you create some value-added e-books in PDF format that you can give away. If you don't have the time or resources to get them written in-house, outsource it to a ghost writer. You'll make back your investment if the leads you obtain are converted into customers.

Several of my clients have looked at me quizzically when I suggested e-books. They didn't think of themselves as publishers before. They believed that e-books are only for people who make their living publishing and selling information. There doesn't seem to be any similar confusion about publishing white papers.

Once they create one, they go on to create several as companions to promotions and offers. Some have also taken their newsletter archives and bundled them into an e-book. It's a very effective way to re-purpose content and can generate new leads.

You Need a Mailing List

Like any good publisher, you need to have a list of customers and potential customers to send offers to. The value of your business is in your mailing list, and for small businesses, this is especially true. Having a list that's both ready and looking forward to receiving offers from you is worth its weight in gold.

But how do you build a list? You need to make a concerted effort. You want a list to contain not only those who have purchased from you, but those who are interested in your products or services and might buy in the future. It is estimated that a customer needs to receive at least seven to nine contacts from you before he will buy. If he can't look you in the eye and evaluate your brick and mortar store, he needs some convincing before he'll spend money with you.

Why Build a List?

Some marketers buy mailing lists, others create their own. You can consider buying lists, but if you are willing to build your own from scratch, you'll probably compile a more responsive group of people. There are many benefits to starting your own list, but it really depends on what you are selling and how reliable you believe any list you might purchase to be. My recommendation would be to start by trying to build your own list.

QUICK Tip

Some benefits to starting your own list are:

- Solid vehicle to market your products
- Special promotions can generate income when you need it
- Subscribers want your information

It is widely believed that when you have created a successful offer you can attribute 40 percent of the success to the list, 40 percent to the offer, and 20 percent to the graphic design. If this is true, your list is a critical part of your business.

Ways to Build Your List

- Put a sign-up link for your newsletter at the bottom of all the emails you send.
- Offer a free issue of your newsletter in exchange for an email address.
- Put a sign-up box on your website home page (make it easy to see).
- Put links to your sign-up page on everything you've published online.
- Create online ads that send users to the sign-up page.
- Sign up for a variety of directory listings.
- Let all your colleagues and friends know how to find you online.
- Comment on blogs similar to your own and link back to your blog or website.
- At the end of your shopping cart purchase, provide a way to sign up for updates (include a check box that gives you permission to contact them with other offers).
- Develop coregistrations or reciprocal links with partners who have your sign-up link on their thank-you page.
- Promote your site at speaking engagements.
- Hand out business cards at trade shows.

Email Software

I've seen much written about building lists, but the key piece of information is often missing. People talk about how to increase the names on your list, but don't talk about what tool to use to set it up.

Alert!

Setting up your email software: You need to use email software that lets you not only send out your promotional materials, but also helps you collect and manage the names on your mailing list. It should keep the names in a database where you can categorize and sort them. You should be able to send emails to people on your list who fit a certain criteria, thereby creating a very targeted campaign.

When you are selecting email software, you have two choices. You can buy and set up mailing list software on your own server, or you can use email software hosted online. There are pros and cons for each. It is possible to collect the names one by one and put them into a database of your own, but I wouldn't recommend it unless you have access to in-house IT people.

Alert!

Online software: Email software hosted online is a much better bet if you are working solo or are starting a small business. You will have someone who safeguards your list for you and to whom you can direct questions. Of course, your software is only safeguarded to the extent that you trust the company you use to host it, so don't cut corners. As you grow, you can increase spending on mailing list services.

Hosted email software, also called an autoresponder, is inexpensive and has all the moving parts integrated for you. I use the autoresponder software from www.1ShoppingCart.com and know others who use and like www.AWeber.com. Look around and choose the tool that suits you best. You may have one that is included with your website hosting. There are also free tools, but they usually have advertising.

Either way, autoresponders are a must-have tool. They do just what it sounds like they do—respond automatically when your customer takes an action you want them to, like typing their email address into your newsletter form. When your user takes this action, it triggers the autoresponder. You set up the autoresponder by determining what response should go with what action; you don't want the email that goes to a customer that just purchased something to say, "Welcome to our mailing list!" for instance.

Autoresponders are everywhere: If you've used the Web for any length of time, I'm sure you've been answered by one. If you've ever emailed a friend or associate and gotten an "I'm on vacation" reply, you've seen an autoresponder.

Autoresponders can be set to any interval, so you can use them to send your customers information in any sequence you choose. If you're teaching an email course, for example, you can set it to send one lesson every week. If you have downloadable software, you can trigger the autoresponder to send it every time someone requests a trial version. You decide when it arrives and what it contains.

Think big: Once your autoresponder is set, it will take the same action over and over until you change it—saving you time and money. No further intervention is required. In fact, if you set it up to trigger a shopping cart, you can be making money too.

I'm often surprised that online businesses of all sizes do not use autoresponders more frequently. Rather than let your leads or customer questions go unanswered, you can use them to show that you are on the job, taking care of your customer's needs.

It's also a great way to deal with repetitive tasks. For example, if a customer signs up for your newsletter, she submits her email address and instantly gets a confirmation of her subscription. If you offer a white paper via email, the user receives a PDF immediately after submitting a request.

Remember, each of your autoresponder emails are written by you, and customized for your target audiences. The key advantage is that you can personalize the message by specifying the respondent's name, product, and any other detail—easy to do when you're setting up the responder. They shouldn't be impersonal. They are great for customer and tech support questions and leave you and your staff free to tackle the more challenging issues.

Also, you don't have to limit the use of autoresponders to customers. You can use it for resellers, vendors, suppliers, or anyone who needs standard replies.

QUICK Tip

What are some ways to use an autoresponder?

- monthly broadcast emails and articles
- tutorials and e-courses by email
- copies of receipts and downloaded instructions
- affiliate information
- vendor registration forms
- phone numbers and details for a teleseminar or webinar

More Tips for Effective Autoresponding

When you send an autoresponder email, you need to personalize it as much as possible. It also needs to be immediately recognizable as intentionally coming from your company, have plenty of white space, use a legible font size for readers of all ages, and, most importantly, the subject line should spell out that this is the information the person requested. If the user has requested a white paper entitled, "Effective Use of Autoresponders," make sure the subject line says that. You don't want your user deleting your email and being annoyed that you didn't respond.

You should also have a place on your website where your customers can get all the information that an autoresponder would email to them, just in case—their email program could label the response as spam, the customer may have entered their email address incorrectly, etc. There are a lot of reasons the email might just have not gone through, so make sure there's a convenient place on your site that answers common questions, such as a FAQ (Frequently Asked Questions) page.

Chapter

Your New Social Media Website

When I took office, only high energy physicists had ever heard of what is called the Worldwide Web...Now even my cat has its own page.

—Bill Clinton

▶ **Why Have a Website?**

▶ **Information "Must-haves"**

▶ **Navigation and Design**

▶ **Is Your Customer in Control?**

▶ **Usability Testing**

As online shopping becomes more and more prevalent, your website, blog, and other online content present your brand to the world. People will form a picture in their mind of how professional you are, how reliable, and how good your product is, based on what they see. They size you up against your competition. This may seem obvious, but when you look around the Web, you see a great deal of variation in how businesses present themselves. No one sets out to show that they are unprofessional, slapdash, or lax, but more than a few let their websites say it for them.

Why Have a Website?

According to the Directory Journal (www.dirjournal.com), a premium search and information service, "online sales have grown in the United States from $12.3 million in 1999 to over $130 million in 2006." They also estimate that "60 percent of 'small merchant companies' have an online presence." Most small businesses today are finding that an online presence really can boost business. Some small retailers confine their search efforts to local search, but the trend to create a website is strong and growing. During the 2007 holiday online shopping season, Nielsen Online (part of the Nielsen Company, a global information and media company) reports that the top five online shopping categories were: (1) clothes/shoes/accessories; (2) books; (3) movies (DVDs/video tapes); (4) music (digital, CDs, tapes); and (5) toys/non-electronic games. The importance of researching products online is growing too. An interesting finding from Jupiter Research in August 2006 reports that 77 percent of online shoppers looked at reviews and ratings before they purchased.

However, just having a website is not enough—you need to have a website that makes people trust you and your products without ever having met you. If someone is considering an online purchase, he needs to feel that yours is a legitimate business that will deliver on its promises. Your credibility and trustworthiness are determined by the professionalism and usability of your website.

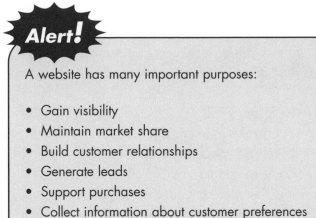

Alert!

A website has many important purposes:

- Gain visibility
- Maintain market share
- Build customer relationships
- Generate leads
- Support purchases
- Collect information about customer preferences
- Sell products and test offers
- Convince vendors, employees, and others to do business with you
- Educate and entertain

Creating a Satisfying Website

It's important to remember that your website is always speaking to three different audiences: (1) your potential and current customers; (2) third parties like vendors, suppliers, and media; and (3) people who have a vested interest in your success—employees and stock holders. You need to pay attention to these five things to support all of these groups:

- Graphics—don't skimp on these; you'll look like an amateur.
- Interesting content—people need to be persuaded with meaningful information.
- Easy navigation—if your user gets lost, he'll leave quickly.
- An easy reliable buying process—this has to work if you intend to make money.
- Help information to support products—this gives the customer immediate satisfaction and prevents you from spending a bundle on support costs.

Website Assessment Quiz

As we proceed through the 7 Step Action plan starting in the next chapter, you will be asked to fill out your worksheet to assess your current reality—the state of your online business. That will let you assess the state of your online business as a whole.

At this point I want you to look specifically at your website. We'll analyze the actual content and weave it into the plan starting in the next chapter.

When you are faced with a website assessment on top of all your other activities, it's hard to know where to start. I created this quiz to help you figure out what needs attention first before you create a marketing campaign. Pause here and fill out the quiz or go to the appendix to fill out the Worksheet called Website Assessment Quiz. (Or you can download it at www.webmarketingforsmallbusinesses.com.)

Figure 6.1: WEBSITE ASSESSMENT QUIZ

To find out if your website is ready for an overhaul, please answer yes or no to the following nine questions:

1. Has the size of your website site grown substantially in the last year?
   YES _____   NO _____

2. Is 25 percent or more of the content outdated or unnecessary?
   YES _____   NO _____

3. Do users have to click more than twice to buy something?
   YES _____   NO _____

4. Are you procrastinating about using social media marketing tactics on your site? (e.g., share this page)
   YES _____   NO _____

5. Does your website design reflect old business objectives—not what you are focusing on now?
   YES _____   NO _____

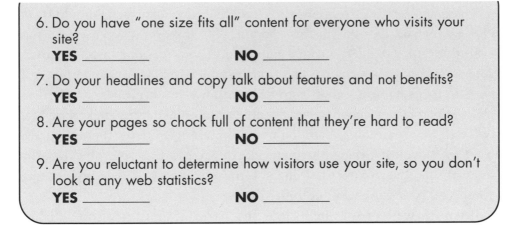

6. Do you have "one size fits all" content for everyone who visits your site?

YES _____ **NO** _____

7. Do your headlines and copy talk about features and not benefits?

YES _____ **NO** _____

8. Are your pages so chock full of content that they're hard to read?

YES _____ **NO** _____

9. Are you reluctant to determine how visitors use your site, so you don't look at any web statistics?

YES _____ **NO** _____

Quiz Answers

Once you have filled out the worksheet, let's look at what the answers mean to you.

If you answered yes to **ALL** the items on your worksheet, work your way through the steps in order: Navigation in this chapter, and Content, Tactics, and Web Analytics as they appear in subsequent chapters.

If you answered yes to items one, two, seven, and eight, your first focus should be on **Content**. (See Chapter 12.)

Within a short time of launch, I'm sure you'll notice that your website is growing—more pages; more content. You start to see where the content holes are and what information your customers are asking for that you haven't supplied.

Within a year, however, the site may start to look and feel like a patchwork quilt. This doesn't mean you are doing anything wrong, but it does require some action. Your business is taking shape and changing to suit the environment and your customers. Unless you make an effort to reorganize and refine, your website will not be as effective and profitable as it could be. As you know, everything moves fast on the Web. Outdated or irrelevant content stands out when users go to find information. The refrain "maybe they won't notice" is dead. If you are just starting out with a new website you have an advantage. You can organize and post content using a plan.

If you answered yes to items three and five, your first focus should be on **Navigation and Design** (in this chapter). It's important for users to find everything they need to make a buying decision. As your business grows, your objectives may change and your product mix will change too. You need to focus on how easy it is to buy and how you can make it effortless. Use the two-click rule whenever possible. Don't make users click more than twice to buy something. You don't want anything to deter them. You also want to ask yourself regularly how well you are meeting your objectives for the website. If you expect nothing in terms of return and measure nothing, you'll get…you guessed it, nothing.

If you answered yes to items four and six, your first focus should be on **Tactics**. (See Chapters 13 and 14.) I've presented a host of tactics, both new and tried and true, that will help you increase business. I want you to pick out the tactics you think will be most effective as you go through the chapters, and plan to implement them first. Give them the time and attention they need before you declare them a success or failure. Don't pick the tactic with the most buzz. Pick the one that suits your business at this moment in time. You'll see that I don't recommend rushing headlong to market on social networking sites unless you understand the tools and know the audience. When you are looking at picking tactics, you should be asking questions like, "What is the best way to increase traffic?" not "How can I fit a newsletter into my busy schedule?" You'll be setting yourself up for failure.

If you answered yes to question nine, your first focus should be on **Web Analytics**. (See Chapter 15.) I firmly believe that you can't really make useful changes to your website if you can't determine how visitors are using it now. Make sure you read that chapter to see how web analytics can make a big difference. At this point in time, measuring your marketing channels is not optional. You need to know where traffic is coming from on your website, blog, etc., and how to increase it. You are in good league with almost every other business owner about feeling somewhat uncomfortable about analytics. Do it anyway. It will mean a great deal to the success of your business, no matter what size.

Figure 6.2: PREPARE YOUR WEBSITE FOR MARKETING

To determine the purpose of your website and decide how best you would like to achieve that purpose, begin by asking yourself these three questions that will help you determine costs and resources needed:

1. What is the main purpose of your website site as it relates to your overall business goals?

Do you sell products or services? If it's services, you probably want people to see your site and phone you for an appointment. If it's a small or inexpensive product, you probably want them to be able to purchase it right from the site. On the other hand, if you sell a big ticket item like a washing machine, you need to supply a lot of technical information like dimensions, weight, shipping information, etc. If you are a local diner, you may want people to print off a copy of your takeout menu and call you. The type of content you have will be dictated by what you are trying to accomplish. When you are budgeting, only create the website you will need for the next six months. In that time, you will determine what else you need based on real world experience.

2. How often does your website need to be updated to serve your customers effectively?

You need to look at this question because it will help you determine your resources. If your products stay constant and prices only change occasionally to support special promotions, then you don't need a full-time person working on your website. If you have new products coming in daily and pictures and descriptions change often, you need to factor that into the support of the site. If you are a very small company or sole owner responsible for website updates, consider a software program like Adobe's Contribute http://www.adobe.com/products/contribute/). Once set up by your webmaster, Contribute allows you to make content changes to your website without having to call anyone. Also make sure your webmaster tells you how to log into your hosting service. You'll need to know that if you hire other people to work on your site. Empower yourself—your website structure is too important to ignore.

3. What back office systems do you need to support your online business?

Think from the outset how simple or complex you need your website to be to support your billing, shipping, etc. If you don't need a complex shopping cart, start with a small one. If you don't have the need for a major invoicing or billing system, don't get one. Start by looking at the least expensive tools that will do the job. As you gain experience, you will find out what you really need before jumping into spending money on something irrelevant.

Alert!

Don't choose out of fear: Be mindful that some of your software choices might be a result of fear. If you think you don't know something, you want the best tool out there to compensate. This would be like purchasing a champion racehorse to ride to the grocery store. Be aware of this and try to look at it objectively.

QUICK Tip

The Home Page Evolution: The classic home page is evolving. Home pages are much more than just a welcome page—they are now like mini-portals to a variety of content, videos, podcasts, etc. Your home page needs to serve as the gateway to all your business's published content. Users have higher expectations today. They want a variety of content formats, easy to read downloads, and check-outs they can quickly breeze through. Your home page should get users to whatever they want quickly and easily.

Information "Must-haves"

Here are the four information "must-haves" for any business website. You don't have to use these category names (although they are considered standard) but you do need to include the information that is supplied within them.

1. About this Company (or About Us)

This is where you tell your potential customers something about your company and yourself. It will help you establish trust and indicate that you are not a fly-by-night business who will take their money and disappear. Here you can be as formal or as comfortable as you want in sharing information. If you have stockholders, you'll have a different message than if you are a small "Mom and Pop" shop. Regardless, you should have your company story on the site to help build a relationship with the customer.

2. Contact information

It is imperative that you have some form of contact information or support clearly listed on your website; visitors will expect an email address and/or phone number, possibly even a physical address. Most small companies today limit their support to providing an email address. If one of your main marketing points is to differentiate yourself from the competition with extraordinary customer service, you need a phone number. You decide what works for you.

3. FAQs (Frequently Asked Questions) and help files

You will start to see the same questions asked over and over again about your company and how to use your website. Compile them all onto a page on your site and answer them—and make sure that you supply the answers to them in a variety of formats—text, audio, video, etc. It's important that you provide as much help information as possible. This will greatly help decrease your support costs and time spent on maintaining the website.

4. Press Room

If you are a very small company, you might be thinking that you don't need this—but social media marketing makes this a necessity. You want to make it easy for others to promote you and tell your story. Compile all your press releases (or write them) for each of your products on this page, and link to any articles about your company, articles you've written for other companies' newsletters or scholarly journals, or any white papers it might be helpful for a journalist writing about you to have. Make people looking for this information feel that you welcome the attention—they'll probably write about you in a more positive light.

Navigation and Design

Being able to navigate easily through your website is perhaps the most important component to your online success—if your customers can't find what they want, how will they buy it? Here's a checklist to help ensure that your website is as easy as possible for the customer to use:

• Make it obvious

Users need to know where they are on the website, where they have been, and where they want to go. Make sure you have a site map.

• Make it consistent

A good way to make it obvious that your company is new to the Web is to change your layout from page to page. Also, don't change your font or colors on a whim. You need consistency—otherwise your website will look like a ransom note, not to mention completely unprofessional.

• Use more than one way to navigate to a destination

Always provide more than one way to get to any section of information. Use a footer if necessary on every page that links to all the most important pages. Readers may not take the path you create for them or expect them to, and they'll miss important information. Make sure they can get to all the most important pages from every screen.

• Follow standard conventions

People have been trained to use websites in specific ways. They expect to see links with a blue underline and your phone number or other contact information clearly visible on every page. Don't be tempted to change conventions like this to be creative. You will only confuse a potential buyer.

CASE STUDY: Three questions for Roger C. Parker, author and designer

1. Has social media marketing changed your approach to online design?

Social marketing encouraged a change in my perspective to a more interactive, less authoritative one-way approach. I now think in terms of topics that spark discussion and comment, rather than just sharing what I know. More important, I am exploring adding "tell a friend," "comment," and "rank this topic" features throughout my websites, rather than just my blogs.

2. You successfully brand across all your online content. Do you have a guiding principle?

Whenever possible, separate graphic design from production. Hire a graphic designer you trust, and ask them to create a set of templates that you can complete yourself as needed so you can do your own production. Have your designer create templates for print projects like newsletters, postcards, and tip sheets.

Likewise, explore online options, like blogs and content management systems, that—once designed—you can update without incurring further costs and delays. Avoid "hostage" situations where the only way you can update your website is to call your designer and wait for them to make the desired changes. You must be able to update your own website if you are to remain competitive.

3. *What is one important tip you would give people designing their first website?*

Instead of focusing on the aesthetics of your website, i.e., colors, graphics, or typefaces, focus on the specific action you want your website visitor to take. If your goal is to encourage visitors to sign up for your monthly e-mail newsletter, for example, your home page should make signing up as irresistible and easy to accomplish as possible.

Avoid home page clutter and distraction. Instead of trying to make a sale, emphasize the value of and describe some of the topics you cover in your newsletter. If possible, include testimonials from your newsletter and white paper readers. Remember, if visitors don't sign up for your incentive and newsletter, you may never get another chance to market to them again!

Additional Resources: Download Roger's "White Paper Design: 16 Easy to Implement Best Practices" at www.designtosellonline. Or, if you want to write a book, download Roger's "Write Your Success: A Step-by-step Guide to Getting Published" report at www.PublishedandProfitable.com.

Is Your Customer in Control?

Once you've built your website, you need to review and make sure it's as user-friendly as possible. Ask yourself who is in control of the information—you or the customer? With the advent of Web 2.0, your answer should always be the customer. The customer needs to look at what they want when they want to and feel in control of the buying process from start to finish.

QUICK Tip

Read up: For solid information about developing and improving your website, check out www.wilsonweb.com for marketing guru Dr. Ralph Wilson's collection of easy to understand web marketing articles and resources. To sign up for his excellent free newsletter "Web Marketing Today," go to http://www.wilson-web.com/wmt/. You'll also want to visit Jakob Nielsen's website at http://www.useit.com/. He's a website usability expert who provides lots of useful information and resources. Also, check out his book, *Designing Web Usability: The Practice of Simplicity.* Another good book is *Web Redesign 2.0: Workflow that Works* by Kelly Goto and Emily Cotler.

Here are five things I recommend you analyze to make sure your site is as effective as possible:

1. Overall marketing message

Is the message clear? Do you use strong copy that clearly describes the benefits of your products or services? In order to feel in control at the beginning of the buying process, customers need to immediately identify the need that you can fill.

2. Product/Service information

Do you provide enough visual information, specs, audio, and video about your product or service? Try to make the customer feel like he has the product in his hand and you are explaining its benefits. Don't skimp on this. You should detail whatever makes your product unique and desirable. If you know your customer needs to see the product from a variety of angles, make sure to supply that. The extra expense is worth it.

3. Price

Have you made your case for the price? Understand that if you have positioned your product at a higher price, you need to communicate the quality and customer service that comes with it—this is particularly important on a website, as you won't be able to reassure the customer in person. You should also sell some smaller, less expensive items that will look very attractive next to the very pricey ones.

CASE STUDY: Making expensive look affordable

If you sell high-end luxury goods, you should definitely keep some smaller, more affordable items in your online store. An August 2007 article by Christina Binkley in the Wall Street Journal *showed how buyers tend to purchase something small from a high-end store as consolation for a very expensive item they can't afford. She says customers "set a new ceiling for a 'reasonable' price."*

If you walk into a store like Tiffany's and see a glass vase for $1,000 that you can't afford, you can comfort yourself with a $100 silver keychain at a fraction of the price. Have you ever wondered why high-end retailers have so many small items you can purchase? Think about it. Before you walked in the store, you never would have contemplated a $100 keychain.

4. Buying process

Is your shopping cart easy to use? Recruit some non-employees to go through the buying process as your team watches. Note where the testers seem confused or something on the site doesn't make it quite as easy for them as it should. Once a user is lost or confused about what to do next, he will abandon his cart and go elsewhere.

Figure 6.4: CONDUCTING A USABILITY TEST

Find three non-employees who aren't users of your products—but could potentially be. Sit each one down in front of a computer and observe as they complete the following four tasks:

1. Tell them your company name and ask them to find your website. Have them tell you what your business sells just by looking at your homepage.

2. Have them pick a product on the site that interests them and write down two benefits they will get from buying it.

3. Tell them to buy the product (you supply the credit card).

4. Let them show you the email or screen that confirms that the product was purchased, the cost charged to the credit card, and the shipping method.

Allow ten minutes for this exercise. Sounds like it should be easy right? I guarantee it will be an eye-opening experience. You will find out if:

• your website is easy to find based on hearing the name

• your product benefits are clearly explained

• your e-commerce solution is fool-proof

• you provide enough documentation so that the customer feels satisfied about the purchase

---

5. Ongoing communication

After purchasing, a buyer wants to feel in control and glad she made the purchase. "Buyer's remorse" can be a symptom of not feeling in control. Make sure to follow-up with the customer and reinforce the good decision of her purchase. Send her an email receipt and a link to additional information on your website that helps her get started using her purchase quickly. If you can get the buyer to start using the product immediately, they are less likely to return it.

Usability Testing

Steve Krug is an important name to know in usability testing—his book *Don't Make Me Think* is a must-read for anyone who wants to do usability testing. It takes a nice, simple approach to the topic. He advocates that you do small frequent tests of your webpages. This is not as easy as it sounds—most people wait a year after a redesign before considering another one. But if you do small tests on a more regular basis, the need for a big redesign is diminished, which can have a very favorable effect on your budget and resources.

Bringing in a Pro

If you decide to call in a professional to evaluate your website, make sure they are capable of doing the following:

- A website evaluation for ease of use and maximization of profits
- An evaluation of your current online marketing plans
- Creation of multimedia online marketing and e-learning materials
- An evaluation of distribution strategies for your channels
- A custom email, newsletter, or other direct response campaign
- A system to improve help documents

CASE STUDY: Tips to remember when you hire outside website designers: Marc Barker, veteran Interactive Producer and Project Manager for Digital Media Works, Inc.

If you plan to hire an outside design firm to create your website, please keep this list handy and make sure they follow these guidelines:

- *Make sure you understand how your client's business mission differs from their website mission.*

- *Understand your client's website mission and weigh all decisions against that statement; question them about the mission, and help them change it if they need to, but make sure that their goals and objectives support that mission.*

- *Don't be all things to all people; don't give your client what they want— give them what their audience needs.*

- *Know your client's customers, their profile/persona, their persuasions. Know how they buy, know what services they need, and stick to a rate structure that serves them.*

- *Help your client to be realistic on e-commerce revenue projections, so they don't expect the website to pay for itself on day one, but make sure they are prepared for success—server load, fulfillment, personnel.*

- *Make sure that clients keep content on their site updated and don't let viewers get bored and not return.*

- *Help your client's website become the authority; entice visitors to return by offering current and relevant content and becoming their online resource to keep them on the site and not stray away. Just as important is to have them share that information and the website with their community.*

Section III

Developing Your
7 Step Action Plan

Chapter  7

The 7 Step Action Plan

A year from now you may wish you had started today.

—*Karen Lamb*

▶ **Why Plan?**

▶ **How to Build the 7 Step Action Plan**

▶ **Buying Online**

▶ **The 7 Questions to Ask Yourself**

▶ **Your Plan**

Shelton State Libraries
Shelton State Community College

I'm sure you've heard this quote from Lewis Carroll's *Alice in Wonderland* many times—"If you don't know where you are going, any road will take you there." Or the equally valid quote from Yogi Berra—"If you don't know where you are going, you might wind up someplace else."

Both quotes imply that defining your goals and planning how you will meet them is the only way to get where you want to go. In this book, I do not recommend that you write a big multi-page marketing plan with executive summaries and sales estimates. The 7 Step Action Plan is **not** a classic marketing plan—because we no longer live in a world that supports classic marketing techniques.

However, even though the traditional models no longer apply, you do have to do some planning or you'll "wind up someplace else." That's why I created my 7 Step Action Plan for the clients of Digital Media Works. They don't have the time or the need for a big detailed marketing plan. But they do have to figure out the essentials—who they will market to and how. This plan helps them grow their businesses and increase revenue. I know it can do the same for you.

Why Plan?

Most of my clients are online business owners who want to progress to the next level—they are either just getting started or are at the point where they know they can sell more and be more successful. So, in creating my 7 Step Action Plan, I put all the online marketing strategies and tactics I know into one place, making sure to include both new and exciting social media tactics and those that are tried and true. I didn't want to exclude things that I know are proven to be successful, but I also know there are new social media tactics that really make a difference.

You have certain overall goals for your business. I want to help you achieve them by pulling out and examining everything you really need to know—and nothing you don't. I constructed this plan to help you figure out if one tactic helps you achieve your goals more quickly than another.

QUICK Tip

Time is money: Internet marketers are harried and overworked. Besides all the big decisions they have to make, they have an onslaught of emails and phone calls that find them wherever they go. Part of developing an effective action plan is figuring out how to spend your time as well as your money the most effectively. We talk about how to analyze this further in Chapter 16.

One other thought to keep in mind—Internet marketing takes patience. It takes time to build an effective search campaign, a well-regarded blog, and a newsletter with a large readership. We think because we can instantly see how many clicks we get that those numbers will grow exponentially—they won't. It's important to consistently write your blog posts and build your website backlinks (backlinks are those sites that reference yours and drive traffic to you). If you do this, you will see dramatic results—but it will take time. The 7 Step Action plan can help jumpstart your efforts.

Alert!

Three-month plans: I know many people recommend three-year or five-year plans for web marketing, but I recommend reassessing your plans at three month intervals. The Web changes too fast for you to assume that some tactic you selected three months ago will still be working. Of course, you need to also make some long-range plans, but keep a constant eye on updating your internet resources.

The dangers of not planning

What if you don't want to plan—you are sure you can wing it and get around to planning later when you have a few more customers. Plan from the start no matter what. There might not be more customers if you don't evaluate what you are doing now.

From my experience, a lack of online planning ensures that you will have:

- Wasted time and money spent on unworkable solutions.
- Lack of "buy-in" from staff and third parties. Unless staff and other participants understand what you are trying to accomplish and where you are going, you will not have their support and participation.
- A website that makes it hard for people to buy your products and generates very little revenue.
- Chaos masquerading as "out-of-the-box" thinking.

How to Build the 7 Step Action Plan

Begin by setting up a file folder system. Take seven folders (online or off) and label them as follows:

1. Niche
2. Brand
3. Story
4. Content
5. Search
6. Tactics
7. Results

Let's begin the 7 Step process by looking at why we are analyzing these steps and not a host of others that you may see in classic marketing plans.

Niche: Most classic marketing plans will ask you to focus on a broad audience. Web marketing in the twenty-first century requires that you narrowly define your audience segments because you are now able to reach them in a way you couldn't pre-Internet. Using concepts like the "long-tail" business model, you are able to find several small well-defined audiences that you can market to instead of one large one. Once you master this process you will be able to recreate it whenever you need to define a new customer segment.

Brand: Defining your brand online is difficult. I put it as the second step in my plan because I know without completing this right up-front, you will not be able to harness the power of your keywords. We will look at how your branding will affect the way you position your website and which tactics you use to reach your audience.

Story: Presenting your website and other content as stories is an important part of the new social media marketing process that many business owners overlook. The more users come to expect entertaining stories from blogs, videos, and podcasts, the more you will be expected to provide this to your customers.

Content: The value of content has risen dramatically as small businesses realize that without materials to educate and sell your products effectively, you are one back button away from another vendor. The competition on the Web is fierce. One way to encourage visitors to return to your website often is to provide them with a constant stream of new and valuable information. Your ability to rank in search engines is also greatly affected. We will look at how to approach building content so that you can compete effectively.

Search: This is something a classic marketing plan would never have, of course. We will tackle how to build a keyword list and figure out how to approach optimizing your website. Search can be a scary topic, but there are simple tips to help you move through the process.

Tactics: I include both social media tactics and the tried and true marketing tactics that will help you jump ahead of your competition. I want you to consider both categories, and I include the social media tactics that I think really make a difference for small businesses now.

Results: Analyzing online results is imperative if you want to grow your online business. We will look at setting up your web analytics and what measures to analyze to encourage profits.

We're now going to start collecting information to complete the 7 Step Action Plan. At the end of each step is a set of conclusions. If you complete them as you work, the plan will put itself together easily and quickly. Don't skip over the conclusions page at the end of each chapter. They were created to help you think through the process. (You can download an entire set of worksheets at www.webmarketingforsmallbusinesses.com.)

Getting started

We'll begin by defining your present day reality—you need to assess where you're starting from. To do this, fill out Worksheet 7.1: Present State. As you fill out this worksheet, think about what your business is, not what you wish it to be—analyze it, warts and all.

After taking this snapshot of where your online marketing stands now on Worksheet 7.1, use Worksheet 7.2 to write down how you are approaching your marketing—your business mindset. Understanding your mindset as you start the planning phase will be helpful.

Worksheet 7.1: PRESENT STATE

1. Take a snapshot of where your online marketing stands now. Describe your current traffic levels and conversion problems.

   _____

   _____

2. Who do I market to now? What are the characteristics of my customers?

   _____

   _____

3. How do my customers perceive me vs. the competition?

   _____

   _____

4. What company stories do I tell now?

   _____

   _____

5. Is my website a good reflection of my company? Why or why not?

   _____

   _____

6. How do customers presently find my online outlets?

   _____

   _____

7. How do I measure my customer's responses?

_____

_____

8. How do I advertise and test my offers?

_____

_____

Worksheet 7.2: **PRESENT MINDSET**

1. What social media tactics and tools do I use today?

_____

_____

2. Do I try to inject innovation and creativity to my business today? If so, how?

_____

_____

3. When I write online content, do I use any specific copywriting rules or guidelines?

_____

_____

4. Do my customers help me shape my marketing message?

_____

_____

5. Do I let users provide their own product reviews, comments, or videos?

_____

_____

> ## QUICK Tip
>
> **Measuring progress:** If you're starting from scratch with a new business, you should still assess where you are in the process, but you should also fill out these worksheets to have a record of where you began. Once you start to make changes, you will have something tangible to compare it to and be able to measure your progress.

Be clear about what your current conversion rate is (if you know it) and what traffic problems you have. (Your conversion rate is calculated by dividing the number of people who visit your site by the number who actually buy something or complete an action requested of them.) Note anything that needs improvement.

Some people ask if you will need to follow the steps in order. If you have done very little planning in the past, I would recommend that you do. If you already have a working plan, you can skip around and concentrate on your weak spots.

Each step builds on the previous one. Only you can determine how much you need to tackle. The key is to make sure that you can answer all the questions when you put the final plan together.

Next, I'd like to look at the steps an online reader takes to make a buying decision.

Buying Online

When someone decides that they would like to purchase a product online, there is likely a process they go through to research information and decide which product is best. They may do any or all of these:

- look at search engine results
- read articles about the topic
- sign up for newsletters relevant to the topic
- listen to podcasts and/or watch video relating to the topic

- look at a variety of products to compare them
- look at comparison engines to review prices
- read customer reviews and ratings
- compare different shipping and delivery options among companies
- see which website makes it easiest to buy at the right price

Will the customer find enough information about your product in all the ways above to select you? As work through the 7 Step Action Plan, remember to keep this list in mind—successful online marketing depends on people being able to easily find you, and favorable information about you, in all these places.

The 7 Questions to Ask Yourself

Now it's time to look at the questions you need to ask yourself to start the 7 Step Action Plan. This will give you an overview of how the 7 Steps fit together.

- ## Step 1. Niche

  Who will I market to?

  You need to start your plan by determining and segmenting your audiences. You'll narrow and target specific demographics and determine a custom message for each.

- ## Step 2. Brand

  How does my customer perceive me versus my competition?

  You'll take a look at your brand and understand how you are positioning your company vs. your competitors.

- ## Step 3. Story

  What do I tell my customer so they understand my company and products?

  You'll learn to create stories and put them on your website to attract the right audience.

- ## Step 4. Content
  Does my website presence accurately reflect my company?
  You'll list the types of content on your website and determine what you are missing.

- ## Step 5. Search
  How will customers find me?
  You'll look at creating a keyword list and search strategy that makes it easy for your customer to find you.

- ## Step 6. Tactics
  What tactics are right for me?
  You can choose from both new and tried and true tactics that suit your goals.

- ## Step 7. Results
  How will I measure my customers' responses?
  Which analytics package or method will you use to track your customers and how do you get started?

Your Plan

The key to a great marketing strategy is a well-defined audience. A well-defined audience is as narrow and specific as you can make it. For most people, it's counterintuitive to think that you can grow your business by narrowing your audience—but this is precisely what you need to do to get your message effectively across to your customers. Become a specialist and your audience will find you more easily because your message speaks directly to them.

Chapter

Step 1. Niche

A niche market is a group of consumers who are a subset of a larger market. Don't confuse this with a market that is small. To be a niche market, your audience needs only to have common demographics or psychographics that define them.

For example, your market could consist of software engineers. To be a niche market they would need to be a subset. They could be female engineers who specialize in developing financial software. The more closely you can define the subset the better you can serve their needs. Learn about their likes and dislikes, what they read, how they spend their time, etc.

Alert!

The Perfect Customer: Some business owners make the mistake of trying to appeal to the widest audience possible. That's a great way to lose everyone at once. When someone reads your headline, they need to feel an instant sense of recognition that you are speaking directly to them. Personalization of the message and a consumer's response to that message are all-important.

Before we start to look at narrowing our audience, we need to look at who you think is your perfect customer. Have you identified him? Are you likely to? If you work too hard to convince your customers that you have the solution to their problem, then you are targeting the wrong customers. This is a key notion. If you are talking to people who have no need for your service, no amount of persuasion is going to work.

One of the great things about marketing on the Internet is that you have customers trying to find you. Your job is to make it easy. If you zero in on the person looking for you, they will be predisposed to buy. It won't be a hard sell. Your goal is to get the customer who believes that your product was specifically created for him.

Three Ways to Help You Find the Perfect Customer

1. Do you know what motivates them to buy?

If you don't, you are missing a big opportunity to connect with them. You can't solve a customer's problem until you know what one business problem occupies the majority of their time. If you have a product targeted to that person, it should be able to solve that problem. If you have a service, then you should have one that works to correct that issue. As you come to understand your target market, you should learn what's important to them and how you can solve their problem.

Many marketers talk about "pain points": the problems that cause the most pain are the ones that get attention first. If a businessperson can ignore a problem without too much pain or risk, they will. You have to find problems that can't be ignored. These are the ones for which people will be actively looking for a solution.

2. Do you know what they hope you will do for them?

Understanding customer expectations is a large part of overdelivering. Overdelivering means that you need to make sure that your customers are overwhelmingly pleased with your products or services. It sounds obvious, but most people settle for customer satisfaction. Overdelivering is the key to making your business grow fast. It encourages word-of-mouth and creates life-long customers.

The way to produce this result is to find out up front what a customer's expectation is. If you find that your customer has a very different outcome in mind, you'll need to talk to them. If you can't do what the customer is asking, walk away. No amount of cajoling is going to make that come out right in the end.

This idea is deceptively simple. If I paint houses and you want a stonemason, it's obvious that you don't want my services. But if I am a dentist and you want your teeth whitened by a method I don't use, it may appear less clear-cut to you—but it isn't.

Niche marketing means that you work to get customers who fit your profile. You want to target people who want their teeth whitened using your preferred method in the timeframe you deliver it. Trying to mess with customer expectations is a recipe for disaster.

The way to find perfect customers is to avoid being "all things to all people." You can't have a perfect customer if you believe everyone is your perfect customer. Once you begin to see the wisdom of niches, you'll see how much easier it makes finding your audience.

3. Find out their information viewing styles.

To find the perfect customer, you'll want to know what information style she prefers (e.g., audio, video, newsletters). This way, you can create content and ads for that medium. For example, check out radio ads and create podcasts if your perfect customer sits in her car all day.

Once you figure out how to find this perfect customer, you can repeat the actions you took to multiply your customer base. The key at this point is not to be tempted to change the message and methods constantly, thus losing what works.

CASE STUDY: Luxury handbags

A great example of a well-defined niche is the online retailer, BagBorroworSteal.com. Their target customer is a woman who covets a collection of the latest luxury handbags to wear to parties and big events. But, owning a collection like that is cost prohibitive for the average consumer. It's BagBorroworSteal.com to the rescue. They will rent her heart's desire for a monthly subscription fee and an additional fee based on which handbag she borrows. This customer likes to be at the forefront of trends, so keeping the bag for a limited time and returning it for something else works perfectly.

You can see how well they've done their job of targeting a very specific consumer. In addition, once they established that target, they added a jewelry line which is also well targeted—if they like expensive handbags, it's likely they love high-end jewelry.

Seven Ways that Creating Niche Audiences Will Benefit Your Business Online

1. Cheaper keywords

By defining the target narrowly, you are going after cheaper keywords sold on advertising search engines like Google and MSN. There's no point in trying to compete with companies who have big advertising budgets. They can afford to buy expensive popular keywords like "online shopping" or "buy online software." Don't waste your money. We'll look at ways to define keywords that really speak to your audience. You'll want to find keywords that are very targeted to your specific audience. For example if you sell footwear for nurses you'd want to use terms like "nurses shoes" and "medical clogs."

2. More targeted traffic

I'm often surprised at the brazen way that online marketing companies say they are going to get you more traffic. You don't want MORE traffic. You want TARGETED traffic that will convert to buyers. Don't get caught up in a numbers game. Just getting large numbers of visits to your website is no guarantee of sales. If you have twenty-five thousand people visit your website each day from a pay-per-click campaign, but very few of them buy, you are wasting your ad dollars. We'll look at this more closely in Chapter 15 on Results.

3. Increased visibility with your audience

You can't buy advertising that will give the same confidence that a referral from a friend will. If you target your audience and provide for their needs effectively, buzz and word-of-mouth will increase among your perfect customers.

4. Instant feedback

One of the best things about online advertising to a niche audience is that you get immediate feedback on how you're doing. People are reading your ads and responding, or they are not. With a niche audience you can use specific phrases. As you start to get results you can further define the keywords by determining if you are getting the exact audience you are targeting. If you were not focusing on a niche audience it would be very hard for you to determine how to reach them, because they would not have specific words and phrases that are only common to them.

5. An understanding about how to reproduce this success for other audiences

Once you understand how to target a specific audience successfully, you will be able to create many more specific groups and understand how to appeal directly to them. This is a valuable skill that will benefit your business no matter what you sell—this way, you know how to expand successfully.

6. You'll be ready for changes in your market.

Keeping this close an eye on your audience means you will feel shifts in their preferences, changes in their lingo, and you can be prepared to support those changes with new products and services. If you were selling a commodity item to a vast audience this would be difficult, but with a niche audience, you have the advantage of being able to monitor their desires closely.

7. You'll have a better understanding and control over your pricing.

Less competition and a clear picture of your audience will help you maintain better margins. You won't be leaving money on the table.

CASE STUDY: Sony targets a niche

Big companies can forget to target their customers effectively as easily as small ones can. Sony introduced its digital book reader, the Sony Reader, in November 2006. It stored up to eighty electronic books and sold for around $300. Hoping to generate buzz, they gave users a hands-on look at the Consumer Electronics Show (CES) in January 2007.

The resultant buzz was small and despite efforts to sell in places like Borders Books, the Sony Reader was still struggling to gain a foothold by September 2007. But, Sony was not ready to give up on it. They believed that it would take time for readers to get used to reading magazines and newspapers from a flat screen and that the market will grow.

So what did they do? Aside from cutting the price by $50 they decided to target two niche audiences:

1. Students, for the back to school season

For this audience they gave everyone registered to their online service credit for one hundred free classic titles like Great Expectations. This appealed directly to students who will be reading the classics for school projects.

2. Frequent travelers, commuters, and those who fly for business

For this audience they rolled out ads in airports and train stations in major cities.

Jim Malcolm, director of marketing for Sony Electronics, was quoted in BusinessWeek in September 2007 as saying, "What we're doing right now is being a lot more targeted. With the introduction of the Kindle by Amazon, they will no doubt be refining their niche even further."

Demographics

To get started narrowing your audience, you want to look at your target audience demographics—their age, gender, income, location, etc. This information is easy to find and easy to sort. By listening to people who buy your category of product or watching buying trends, you can begin to see groupings. If you sell a gender-specific product, you will begin to see age patterns. Take what you know about your audience and look for the other ways in which they are connected.

The key is to be able to define your market in a one- or two-sentence statement. If you sell organic bath products out of Maine, you might define your audience as "female spa owners with businesses with over $2 million in sales, located in New England, who only use and sell natural products." From this description, you can then begin to delve into information that reveals what is unique about this group.

Psychographics

Once you feel that you have collected demographic information, you want to look at their psychographics. This concept is a bit more complex than demographics—it deals with people's thoughts and feelings, so it's harder to measure than concrete data. However, it's very valuable information; it can help you begin to understand why your customer buys your product and how he thinks and feels about it, which can be a powerful way to refocus your marketing.

The best way to get this type of data is to survey and talk to your customers and others who buy similar products. The biggest mistake is not asking. If you rely solely on what you think, rather than what THEY think, you'll have a warehouse full of unsold products. You want to interview your customer support people and see what they are hearing from customers, both good and bad.

QUICK Tip

Casing the competition: To understand how the customer views your competitors you should look at their marketing materials and see what they think is important for their customers to understand.

As you build a profile, you begin to understand what your customer's hot buttons are. In addition, you should be looking closely at your web analytics to understand what pages your customers frequent and why. This is known as behavioral targeting. You'll want to consider visitors' interest in one specific product of yours over another and find out why. This information can tell you which of your products are successful and why, and you can take that information and apply it to all of your products and services.

Alert!

Some questions to ask yourself about your audience:

1. How do they gather online information to make a buying decision? Are there specific blogs, online news, or social bookmarking sites they frequent?
2. How does the competition view this audience?
3. Does one gender prefer my product by a wide margin?
4. Is there a specific age group that buys my product?
5. What price would they consider paying for my product or service?
6. How can I build an online mailing list to target these people effectively?

Using Personas

Once you have defined your niche and gathered both demographic and psychographic information about them, you need to use it to create a customer profile in order to build targeted marketing tactics. The dictionary definition of "persona" is an actor's portrayal of someone in a play, but we're using it to describe a profile for your target customer. To be effective, you need to create several personas, one for each of your niche markets. Personas are not defined by an easy demographic description, but by their behavior and the goals they want to achieve by using your product. When you establish customer goals, you can build a marketing profile that will assist you in every part of the buying process. Basically, you know what they want and how they want it, so you can tailor your business to provide it. For this strategy to be effective, your staff needs to feel that your personas are real people and sell specifically to them.

More on personas: Alan Cooper introduced the concept of personas in his 1999 book *The Inmates Are Running the Asylum* to assist designers creating software. At first, some people may resist using the concept of personas because they feel silly giving a name (and if you prefer, a face) to a customer profile. One client said that he felt it was like "creating imaginary friends." But Cooper makes it clear that nothing could be further from the truth: "They are not real people, but they represent them...We don't so much make up our personas as discover them as a byproduct of the investigation process." You are uncovering who your real customers are, not making them up from whole cloth.

Personas force you to focus on creating the right marketing message for the right customer. The goal of using personas is to designate one "person" to represent an entire customer group. Rather than trying to be all things to all customers at once, you can focus on making sure that the information path and the data that that one "person" needs is available to them. You can then move to the next persona and make sure you are meeting his needs. It's methodical and helps you frame your website more efficiently.

When you are getting started creating personas, start with a small number, maybe two or three. You can get more expansive later, but for now you want to stay focused. The key is to focus on the goals your customers have in using your product. You can then decide how to meet those goals with your information and web navigation.

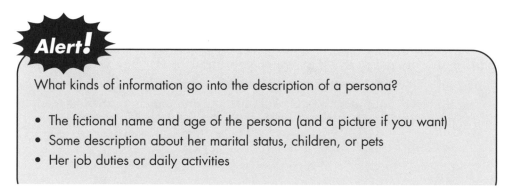

Alert!

What kinds of information go into the description of a persona?

- The fictional name and age of the persona (and a picture if you want)
- Some description about her marital status, children, or pets
- Her job duties or daily activities

- What goal she has in using your product
- How and where she consumes information on the Web
- Some personal information about habits or attitude

Figure 8.1: **CONCLUSIONS WORKSHEET—NICHE**

1. Describe your niche audience's demographics in one sentence.

_____

_____

2. Describe your niche audience's psychographics.

_____

_____

3. Describe your perfect customer in detail.

_____

_____

4. What groups will you create for your mailing list?

_____

_____

5. List the personas you have created and give the characteristics for each.

_____

_____

Chapter

Step 2. Brand

The world is changing. Networks without a specific branding strategy will be killed...
—Barry Diller

- ◗ **Branding Basics**
- ◗ **Positioning**
- ◗ **Crafting Your Brand and Positioning**
- ◗ **Taglines**
- ◗ **Logos**

If you have an established brand, social media marketing dictates that you aggressively own it. It needs to be obvious, repeatable, and ready for storytelling by the customers who will carry your message. You need to commit to it and make sure your employees do too. But, what if you don't have a strong brand, or one at all? If this is the case, you need to decide how to present your company and what it stands for.

Branding Basics

Branding can be a complex topic. There are agencies whose sole job it is to work everyday to improve a company's brand. Here are some of the basic elements you need to know about branding that really matters to you as small business owner:

1. Identity

Your brand needs to signify something specific in the customer's mind. If she's unclear or confused about what you sell and the benefits of it, your branding is meaningless. And if your identity changes based on who you are talking to, you don't really have an identity. That doesn't mean that you can't appeal to a variety of niches, but it does mean that you have to identify how you communicate that appeal to each one specifically.

2. Consistency

If your product makes a promise to your customer, you have one real chance to satisfy it or their interest is lost. And each subsequent product they order needs to also satisfy or exceed that promise.

3. Trust

If a customer is loyal to your brand, you have to meet their expectations every time or you lose their trust

4. Pricing

If a customer believes you are providing a higher-quality product, you can charge more, but you need to protect that impression and nurture it. Your price should be determined by the quality of and demand for your brand.

What's different today?

Your brand is the image that customers have when they think about you. A weak brand communicates to the customer that they should use caution when buying your products. If you don't have a clearly defined brand, customers don't know what to think of you at all. In addition, the forces at work today that occupy people's minds are plentiful. Marketers today have to deal with two factors when crafting your brand that your pre-Internet predecessors did not:

1. Too much clutter.

There are an unlimited number of commodities available to a customer today—shampoo, for instance. There are hundreds of brands of shampoo for a consumer to choose from. People can even get them sent overnight. Unless you can figure out how to rise above the clutter, you are unlikely to sell much shampoo.

2. Customers shape the brand.

Marketers need to listen to the customer to understand how they perceive the brand. It's crucial that you do this as you prepare each step of your action plan. You will not be able to dictate your position. You will need to mold and shape it with feedback from your customer; if you don't, they'll find a company that will.

This is both good and bad. If your customers love your product and evangelize it, you have a potent sales force. If they find its weak spots and advocate changes, you are forced to listen. The good news is that you will hear from them, and whether it's good or bad news, you'll know exactly what your target audience needs to be happy.

Positioning

The concept of positioning is basic to brand building and growing a business online or off. It is the **position** that a customer holds in his mind about a particular brand, business, idea, or anything that can be ranked. **It is not about the product, it is about the perception of the product in a potential customer's mind**. For example, if a consumer thinks Coca-Cola is best, then it holds the first position in the list of soda choices. Unless the customer is given a reason to try something else, they'll always buy Coca-Cola.

More on positioning: The term "positioning" was coined by Al Ries and Jack Trout over thirty years ago. To learn more about this topic check out their book, *Positioning*, and *The New Positioning* by Jack Trout.

In 2008, the topic is more important than ever. The millions of businesses on the Web all compete for the few positions in your mind.

The classic positioning example is Avis Car Rentals' use of the slogan "We're Number Two, We Try Harder" referring to the position they held in the minds of consumers. They were number two behind Hertz, which was the most popular car rental service. The goal was to get you to rank car companies by a different list. Not the most well-known, but the list of car companies that try harder. You probably didn't have a ranking for that in your mind. They created that list and put themselves at the top—"We're number one in 'trying harder' so our service will be better."

Alert!

Be inimitable: Make sure your position is hard for a competitor to copy. A high barrier to entry makes competitors think long and hard about trying a "me too" approach. A high barrier to entry refers to the notion that the harder it is for a competitor to start and operate a business just like yours, the less likely he is to try it.

Crafting Your Brand and Positioning

Begin the branding process by determining the most simple and obvious features and benefits of your product. There are millions of messages assaulting consumers every day—you need to be clear and concise. Here are some mistakes to avoid:

- Don't try to invent a concept that isn't already in your customer's head. You want to develop a position that is clear in the mind of your customer, not a new idea—you need to emphasize what makes your product better than the ones like it. A clear differentiation makes it easy to decide to buy one product over another.
- Don't make it complex. The idea is to appeal to something instantly understandable. If you have a complex product, try to simplify it to the main benefit.
- Don't stick to features—go for benefits.
- Don't try to get it perfect; test and see how ideas are received before you decide. Once you launch, your customers will help you shape the brand.

Six Questions to Help Develop Positioning

1. Am I first?

If you are the first product addressing a specific need in the market, using that fact as your positioning is a no-brainer. However, in industries crowded with all sorts of variations on a theme, this is unlikely to happen. You need to think about how you can define yourself as first. Are you the first to offer "customer service plans with unlimited calls?" If you define your own category, you can be first.

2. Am I the biggest?

Don't worry if you're not. Find some way to position yourself against those attributes like Avis did. They weren't the biggest; they were the ones who tried harder. If you aren't the largest online retailer of software in your field, perhaps you are the one who is "rated number one in customer service."

3. Am I the only one in my category?

Again define the category so that you can be the only one. For example, "we are the ONLY shoe company that offers two additional packs of free laces with our sneakers." Find something that will set you apart and use that in all your advertising.

4. Do I have credentials to support my claims?

Do you belong to a certifying association or have degrees that support your services? Have studies been done by outside agencies to support your assertions? Being the most qualified in your category is great positioning.

5. Do I state quantifiable differences?

If you can determine that your vacuum is three times more likely to pick up dirt and dust than your competitor's, that's important. If the flavor of your gum lasts 50 percent longer than the competition, mention it. If you can be specific, you can stick in the customers mind. But don't stop here. Younger customers will perceive this as "old school." Look beyond the statistics to the feelings—your gum lasting 50 percent longer means saving your gum money for something else.

6. Can I redefine my product category?

Perhaps you can rethink how your category will be used by your customers. Starbucks differentiated themselves from all the other coffee shops by becoming a place for entrepreneurs to work when away from their homes. Other diners and coffee shops had the same opportunity, but didn't provide the atmosphere and wireless support to make that happen.

QUICK Tip

Selling a complicated product: If you sell a product or service that is very complex, you might not be able to pin down overt differences between you and your competitors. The good news is that on the Web you have the opportunity to provide as much supporting material as your customer needs in all formats.

Here are some things you can try to help clearly explain your position to consumers:

- Make sure your customer comes in contact with the message several times before you expect them to buy. Send them a newsletter that explains it, show them a video that demonstrates it, etc. Complexity becomes easier to understand the more times you see it. If you build this into your brand marketing, you will see better results.

- Break down the complexity into manageable chunks. This is called "chunking" information—breaking down the information into bite-size pieces. If you are selling a complex technical product you can have information in various formats about its benefits, then how it's made, then how you install it. This way it can be consumed over time.

- Let the customer know that they will need some time to understand all the components. Fast and easy is the byword for marketers, but pretending it's fast and easy when it isn't only makes the customer feel stupid—and unsatisfied. Be honest about the complexity and make sure you provide enough customer support to make it easy for your customers.

Taglines

A good tagline is critical for your website. You will carry it on all your marketing channels—newsletter, blog, website, online communities, etc. When people land on a website, they quickly search around on the page to answer the question, "What is this about?" A good tagline can answer that question in one second (which is the amount of time you have to get someone's attention) by letting the reader know what you do. If you capture their attention, they will look around some more. If not, they are off to the next site. If it's confusing, they won't stay.

Creating a great tagline requires some thought and time to let your ideas incubate and grow. You need to brainstorm to develop your tagline, so I suggest you create a Mind Map. Here are some ideas to get your map started:

- Brainstorm words that describe the solutions you provide. Now that you've defined your niche audience, you know who your target market is and what their problems are. Make a list of the problems and then from that create keywords that define solutions. If you feel stuck, start the sentence with, "We help you _____," and then put it down on the map. Write down as many words as you can think of.

- Add words that explain the unique value of your company. Try not to list words that are so general that they are almost meaningless. For example, trustworthy and reliable are great attributes, but not for your tagline.
- Add words that have emotional appeal. Think about what your customers want to feel when they buy your product. Do they want to feel smart, self-assured, like a trendsetter, like an insider? Collect those words on the map.
- When you are done, look at your map and try to find patterns. That's why Mind Maps can be so helpful. They will help you create groups of words that go together.
- Print out the map and let the ideas percolate. When you come back to it, try to add more ideas until you have some taglines you like.

Test the taglines on others and ask for their reaction. You'll know when you have one that fits—it will feel good to you and people will respond positively to it. Then you have to see how your customers react. Taglines evolve over time, and will be tweaked depending on what customers tell you and each other. For instance, Avis has dropped the "We're number two" from their tagline and just uses "We try harder."

Logos

Creating a logo for your company is serious business. It doesn't have to be costly, but it requires professional help. How many times have you visited a website only to be greeted by a cheesy clip art logo? Did this instill confidence in you about the quality of their work? Did you wonder if the business was going to be around long enough to support your guarantee? A poor logo can lose business for you before your visitor ever reads a word.

Since identity design is not an area that most business owners are familiar with, they tend to land on one side of the spectrum or the other—either they spend a great deal of money on an identity campaign out of fear that they will look amateurish, or they ignore it altogether and hope it won't matter. Identity design includes more than just your logo. It is the fonts, style, and look of all your marketing materials. Obviously, a middle ground would be much more effective. People will notice your "look" and your positioning will be affected by their reactions to it.

Five Tips for Hiring a Professional to Design Your Brand Identity

1. **Before you speak to any designer, be clear about your target audience and positioning.** Your designer will want to know this and if you are confused or unclear, the results will be less than you hoped for. Don't call designers hoping they will figure it out. They expect you to be an expert in your business so they can be an expert in theirs. If they are willing to work with a loose description, be wary.

2. **Think about colors and presentation.** Do you want your brand to appear very formal? Are you a service business with professional certifications and industry awards? Let your designer know. You don't want branding that says you are a "whimsical" accountant, even if it looks cool. Show them examples of brands you admire.

3. **Look at the designer's online portfolio.** If you don't like what you see, you won't like your custom design any better.

4. **When you speak with the designer, make sure they have a marketing sense.** I'm not saying that they have to be marketing experts, but there are designers out there who care more about the aesthetic appeal of their design than how it fits the customer's business. Don't be bullied.

5. **Don't expect good design work to be cheap.** Be prepared to spend a reasonable amount. Look at a variety of designers before you finalize your budget. It's hard to change a brand identity once you create it, so bear that in mind when you are making your choice. If you feel you are compromising, you'll never be happy.

Figure 9.1: CONCLUSIONS WORKSHEET—BRAND

1. Describe what your positioning is. (First, biggest, etc.)

_____

_____

2. Write down the list of solutions you offer your client.

_____

_____

3. What is your tagline? (attach your Mind Map to this sheet) Why did you choose it?

_____

_____

Chapter  10

Step 3. Story

The difference between the right word and the almost right word is the difference between lightning and a lightning bug

—*Mark Twain*

▶ **Why Do We Love Stories?**

▶ **What Makes a Good Story?**

▶ **Types of Stories**

▶ **Stories Your Customers Care About**

▶ **Capture Your Success Stories**

Everywhere you look, you see information about business storytelling. If you're wondering why there has been a renewed interest, it's because the Web has presented us with an inexhaustible supply of stories and an equal number of ways to tell them. For instance, YouTube has enabled anyone with a video camera to post their story for all to see.

Why Do We Love Stories?

Our love of stories is hard-wired. We learn as infants how to make sense of the world through stories. As we grow, we use our left brain to analyze and study details and our right brain to experience emotions and discern patterns. Stories engage both sides of our brain. They help us remember events in a way that reading a factual account could never do.

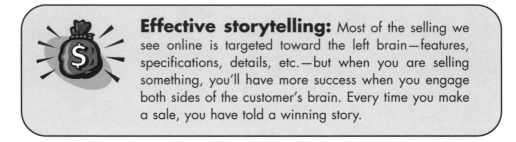

Effective storytelling: Most of the selling we see online is targeted toward the left brain—features, specifications, details, etc.—but when you are selling something, you'll have more success when you engage both sides of the customer's brain. Every time you make a sale, you have told a winning story.

When we talk about stories in a business setting, it's important to understand that they are not fabricated from whole cloth—at least not usually. EBay founder, Pierre Omidyar, often told the story that he started his company to help his girlfriend buy and sell items from her Pez dispenser collection. He now admits he "embellished" that story, but people delighted in telling it. It appealed to their sense of surprise and romance.

The stories you gather about your company should be true and represent something unique. You need to give them time and attention. Stories should explain why your company is a business your customers want to associate with.

The Benefits of Storytelling

To understand storytelling for business, we need to look at its benefits. Storytelling helps us:

- express our emotions
- persuade others
- talk about provocative subjects
- make sense of bad things that happen
- develop role models who inspire us
- sell things

Stories help your company and products appeal to people in a memorable way. To create good business stories, you need to understand what makes a story worth listening to.

The stories you need: Annette Simmons, author of *The Story Factor*, says that there are several business stories you need to be able to tell. She includes "Who am I?" and "What's my vision?" These types of stories help people understand your business and your message. They become doubly important when you want to persuade people to buy from you. On the Web, this is true because the delete key and back button are ever present.

What Makes a Good Story?

Everyone tells stories, but not every story is worth listening to. Unless you have an established relationship with the storyteller, you are apt to give her roughly five to ten seconds to interest you. After that, you turn your attention to whatever is next.

QUICK Tip

Appeal to their emotions: When the *Harvard Business Review* asked well-known screenwriter Robert McKee how he persuades people, he said that one way was to argue with someone until hopefully they agreed. But, he said, "A much more powerful way, is by uniting an idea with an emotion."

If you have ever heard employees proudly tell "how our company got started" stories, they generally cast the owner or founder as a hero who overcomes the odds to accomplish something. For example, "Joe was bankrupt when he started Acme Widgets. His family was desperate. Still, he mortgaged his house and sold his car to start the company." The story has a satisfying ending because Joe and his company are thriving.

Another typical variation on that company story would be for Joe to slay a "villain" of some kind. "The Mal Widgets Company tried to thwart Joe by stealing his customers, but with perseverance and hard work, Joe won them back." You can see that the stories are simple, yet effective. Each story has a beginning, middle, and end. The reason they work is because they appeal to the emotions of consumers; after hearing these and understanding what motivates you, consumers will root for you.

Negative Stories

What about negative stories—are you aware of them? You will quickly learn that negative stories about your company from customers can be deadly. On the Web you see many examples of this when you look at product review sites like epinions.com whose headline says they are "unbiased reviews from real people." What that means to you is that regardless of your size, your customers have outlets to air their grievances about you—and they will. You need enough responses from satisfied customers to counteract the damage, because people will be researching your company online before they buy.

User stories impact you both online and off. You want to have positive stories your customers feel compelled to tell when they talk about your products or services. You also want to have stories your employees can tell about how the company got started or what your vision is for the future. It should be a story that means something to you, your employees, and your listener. If they tell a story that does not fit with the company's image or products, a sale may be lost and an image destroyed for that customer.

The challenge is that you can't **make** people tell a story that isn't true. You have to listen to the stories being told both inside and outside your company and work to bring out your authentic beliefs.

Everyone has a story that will be told: When *Fortune* magazine lists its top one hundred companies to work for, you can look at the list (Google is #1 for 2007) and realize that for big companies, everyone knows the stories being told. As a small business owner, you believe that your story is too small to be heard. On the Web, no story is too small to tell, and one of your employees or customers will tell it. Make sure it says what you want it to.

CASE STUDY: The real J. Peterman

A humorous example of storytelling in business is employed by the J. Peterman Catalog. You may recall that a fictional J. Peterman Catalog Company, was featured on the TV show Seinfeld *as the place where Elaine Benes worked. An actor created the fictional J. Peterman—but there is a real J. Peterman, and a real catalog.*

The products in the real-life catalog are accompanied by fun stories to evoke a mood and sell the product. Peterman is quoted on his website as saying "People want things that are hard to find. Things that have romance, but a factual romance, about them."

In the catalog, the products have small vignettes that engage the reader. For example, one of their silk dresses is accompanied by the following description: "Tea at the Plaza, 1935. You and your fiancé have an understanding: if you don't use the word 'Depression,' you'll never see evidence of one." It's a device that works very well to engage customers and engender emotion, thus stimulating both the left and right brain.

Types of Stories

Most people don't equate what they or their employees know about the company as stories worth repeating. But that's not true. You can tell stories about how you invented your product, how you improved it, who influenced you, etc. There are great stories locked in your head and you need to get them on paper. To help you get started, you need to understand how to structure a story.

In their great book, *Made to Stick*, Chip Heath and Dan Heath pondered how many story types exist. They wrote that, after investigating and boiling it all down, there were really only three types of stories:

- The challenge plot, which describes overcoming the odds
- The connection plot, which involves people who help others regardless of the differences between them
- The creativity plot, in which someone solves a problem or innovates in some unique and notable way

When you are looking for stories to tell your customers, you need to be able to determine which of the three types of stories you are trying to tell. That will help you create a clear, compelling story line.

QUICK Tip

Tell more stories: To do a quick check of where you are now with your storytelling, go to your website and pick out all the stories you tell. My guess is that you'll only have the "about us" story. You need more.

Stories Your Customers Care About

In his book, *The Power of Story*, Jim Loehr says that all good storytelling consists of three ideas: purpose, truth, and action. In order to create meaningful stories for your products—aside from deciding the plot—you need to know what your purpose is for telling the story, that it rings true, and that the actions it describes effectively support your reason for telling it.

Before you start developing your stories, make sure you know the answers to the following questions

• What do my customers worry and care about?

These are the topics about which you want to focus your stories. If you sell tennis equipment and know that customers fear injury and downtime, you should focus stories on how your products increase stamina and prevent injuries.

• What are my customer's expectations for my product or service?

Customer expectations are key. If you know your customers expect your product to last forever, you can offer a "lifetime replacement" in exchange for shipping and handling. The story you are telling is that you back up your product 100 percent.

• Which media do my customers prefer? (video, audio, text)

Obviously, if you sell audio equipment, you know that podcasts are the way to go. But no matter what you sell, you should always survey your customers and check your web analytics to see which types of media they respond to.

• Where do they get their information? (magazines, newspapers, blogs, etc.)

If you know where they get their information, you'll know where to place your stories.

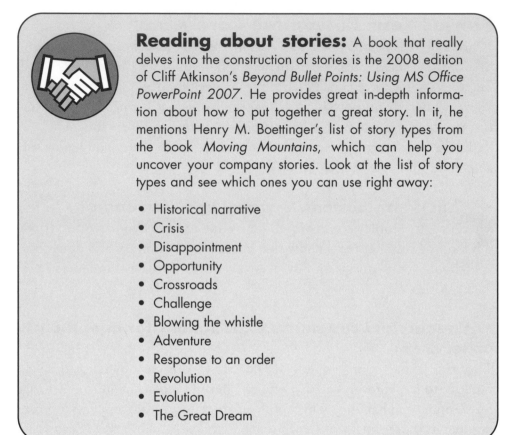

Reading about stories: A book that really delves into the construction of stories is the 2008 edition of Cliff Atkinson's *Beyond Bullet Points: Using MS Office PowerPoint 2007*. He provides great in-depth information about how to put together a great story. In it, he mentions Henry M. Boettinger's list of story types from the book *Moving Mountains*, which can help you uncover your company stories. Look at the list of story types and see which ones you can use right away:

- Historical narrative
- Crisis
- Disappointment
- Opportunity
- Crossroads
- Challenge
- Blowing the whistle
- Adventure
- Response to an order
- Revolution
- Evolution
- The Great Dream

Metaphors

Any section on storytelling would not be complete without a mention of metaphors. As screenwriter Robert McKee said, storytelling is about uniting an idea with an emotion. Metaphors are comparisons that describe something for your readers by calling it something else. For instance, calling a stubborn person a "mule" is a metaphor, as is describing a lovely girl as a "flower." Metaphors can help you link ideas and emotions because they are symbolism everyone understands, and people already have associations with those symbols that evoke emotion.

For example, if you are a full-service design firm, you could describe yourselves with: "We are the gourmet chefs of the design world." Your competition can be the "fast food employees" who turn out everything the same way regardless of need. Of course, you'll want to stay away from overused metaphors that are meaningless and signal a lack of imagination, such as:

- a painful lesson
- a shining example
- boiling mad
- a deep dark secret

You get the idea. No one will pay attention if it's something they've heard a thousand times before.

QUICK Tip

Finding your metaphors: Listen for metaphors when you are explaining things to your customers—you may already be using them everyday and just haven't noticed. Also, listen to how customers describe your products and services. They could come up with powerful metaphors to describe your work for you. Finally, ask your sales people to tell you metaphors that work for them when they are pitching your product.

Capture Your Success Stories

As we discussed, your company stories already exist. What you need to do is to capture them as they happen and publicize them. Capturing them is not hard—it just requires some preparation. If you have customer support staff, make it part of their job to report stories about customers, both happy and not so happy. Make sure your employees understand that they have the authority to satisfy your customers (set a dollar limit if appropriate) and tell them you want to see how they resolved the situation. Do the same with your sales people. The key here is to make it easy to capture the story so you'll have it when you need it.

Of course, you can use the customer stories as testimonials on your website. But, you want to do more than that. You want to make sure that everyone in your company can repeat them when the need arises. On a sales call, when someone expresses a concern, it's more effective to say you've faced that problem and describe how it was handled.

Figure 10.1: CONCLUSIONS WORKSHEET—STORY

1. Describe one story that you want everyone associated with your company to tell. Which of the three plots does it contain—challenge, connection, creativity?

   _____

   _____

2. Develop a story about why you created your business. Which of the three plots does it contain—challenge, connection, creativity?

   _____

   _____

3. List some of the metaphors you will be using.

   _____

   _____

4. How do you plan to capture success stories?

   _____

   _____

Chapter

Step 4. Search

Think like a wise man but communicate in the language of the people.

—*William Butler Yeats*

Keywords are the words people use to find you online—they are the words that search engines such as Google use to direct people who are looking for that word to you. They are the way you build your company's communication pipeline to your customers. It's often been said: "If search engines can't find you, you don't exist." To prevent yourself from being invisible, let's look at some keyword basics.

What You Should Know About Search Engines

Let's look at the search engine landscape. comScore, an Internet market research firm, reported in April 2007 on the percentage breakdown of most used search engines:

- Google had 48.3 percent of the searches
- Yahoo had 27.5 percent
- MSN had 10.9 percent
- Ask.com had 5.2 percent
- Time Warner had 5 percent

Therefore, it is most important to submit your website to be spidered by Google, Yahoo, MSN, and DMOZ (the main directory of websites). The term "spidering" refers to the action the search engine takes, crawling around the Web and getting updated information.

QUICK Tip

Using Google to find all your online info: You can use Google to search for specific information about your website. Type the following into the Google search box as indicated:

"Site:Your URL"—Shows the pages indexed for your site. (For example, typing "Site:digmediaworks.com" into the search page reveals all the pages indexed for my website.)

"Link:YourURL"—Shows pages that link to your site.

"Info:YourURL"—Shows several lists of information about your site.

Organic vs. Pay-Per-Click

Organic lists of search results and pay-per-click (PPC) are two different results from searching a keyword—the organic comes from the popularity ranking from the search engine and the PPC are the paid ads that result. Both are important. The organic list of search results is displayed on the left side of the screen; the sponsored ads (PPC) are on the right.

In the organic list, the order is based on that search engine's algorithm (formula) for displaying the most popular items at the top. It's important to understand that regardless of whether you buy any sponsored ads in Google or any other search engine, you will (hopefully) be spidered and displayed in the organic list as well. Search engine optimization of your website makes it easy for search engines to find and spider your site. The quality of your search engine optimization (SEO) determines how quickly you are spidered and where you are on the list.

To be on the right side of the page in the list of sponsored ads, you need to set up a PPC campaign in Google, or the search engine of your choice. You bid on the keywords to have your ads displayed on the search results. In this section we discuss how to select keywords and then look at using them in PPC campaigns.

Why Do Keywords Matter?

Keywords matter to you in four important ways:

1. They help interested customers find you.
2. They help level the playing field. You can compete against bigger, better-known companies by purchasing the same keywords they use and usurping their customers.
3. They help develop the content on your website—when you've determined your keywords, you know what must be included and you can plan for it.
4. They help you meet your business goals by taking a strategic approach to your search campaigns.

As you get started, it's important to understand that your website and any online content you create needs to appeal to your customers and be optimized for search engines, so that people are directed toward your website. This means that when you are creating content, you need to be aware of the keywords that help people find you and use them as much as possible. That's why whenever you create online content of any kind you want to know what keywords you will be optimizing for.

Six Steps to a Keyword List
Follow these steps to start developing a good keyword list:

1. Brainstorm a list.
Start by brainstorming. Put down your company name, product names, and other pertinent company names. Include any words or phrases that relate to your products. Ask staff, friends, and colleagues to add to the list.

QUICK Tip

Pillage pop culture: Aaron Wall, CEO of SEOBook.com, suggests some additional fun and unique ways to seed your keywords list. He recommends that you check out the junk mail you receive to see what words are commonly used by people selling things. People are very familiar with these words and they will come to mind quickly when they're searching for something online.

If it's on TV, it's a popular keyword or phrase. Try the Yahoo Buzz Index to see what you can find. You should also look at the Amazon and *New York Times* Bestseller's lists. There are lots of terms big in pop culture that relate to your business, and you can use them to generate traffic to your site.

2. Use a keyword suggestion tool or two.
Next, you need to analyze the list that you've brainstormed to find real-world searches that people use. This is something that people often miss. The brainstorm list is just a list of **guesses**—until you confirm that people actually use those words to search, they are just a list of possible keywords. Without verifying that people use it, you might include a word that seems right but is not one that searchers actually use.

The quickest way to confirm keywords is to use a keyword suggestion tool. One of the most commonly used ones is the Overture Search tool at http://inventory.overture.com/d/searchinventory/suggestion/. A keyword suggestion tool helps you determine whether your guesses match reality. It will return a list of those words and phrases that have actually been searched earlier in the year. It will also tell you how many times they have been searched in a given period. This is your real-world proof that people are searching on these terms.

Another good online tool is at www.Wordtracker.com. Many professional SEO experts use it because it shows you how many people are actually searching for a particular keyword and what related terms exist. (They have a free trial, and then if you want to subscribe, there is a small fee based on an interval you choose.) They have lots of good information there as well.

3. See what keywords your competitors are using.

You can find a competitor's keywords by going to their site and clicking on "View" on your browser toolbar. Then select "Source." This will bring up a screen with a lot of confusing looking text, but don't be put off. Look at the top few lines and find "keywords meta tag." That's the list of keywords used for the site. Remember, this is just part of your brainstorm—just because your competitors are using these words doesn't mean they've been proven effective. More research is needed.

4. Identify your niche words and phrases.

This is important if you have more than one niche and you run a targeted ad for one of them. You want to make sure you use those words that you identified for that segment. If your niche audience is comprised of gamers, you'll want to target different segments in each ad. For example, if you have a female segment, you will use keywords like "female gamers," "female players," and "female games" on your list.

5. Determine relevance and importance to your business.

The final step before you start using your list is to look at it for relevance and importance. Do a final pass and make sure that the keywords and phrases are not too general and truly are ones that are appropriate for your business. Getting a lot of traffic with no potential sales is a waste of time and resources.

6. Begin using and testing your list.

Now that you have a list of keywords, use them to optimize your website. If you already have some keywords and are using them in a Google AdWords campaign, you can use the Google Keyword Suggestion tool to find more keywords and test them.

What you are trying to do is find the most direct words, phrases, and even acronyms that potential customers will use to find you. If you haven't run a PPC campaign, you'll need to find out how much you will have to bid to use those keywords (more on that below). Testing is a key part of this process and can be taken in two steps. First you want to test whether the keywords you put into a search engine actually bring up searches that are right for your product. That's an "eyeball" test and can be done by going through and performing several searches. The second step is testing whether the campaigns you set up with the keywords actually succeed in bringing traffic.

QUICK Tip

Five tips for selecting keywords:

1. Don't pick broad generic words that cost a lot and yield no tangible results. You'll never come up on the first page of search results if you use the word "shopping" for example. There are 860 million citations ahead of you.

2. Use niche phrases whenever possible. At the time of this writing, three- and four-word phrases work very well for targeted traffic.

3. Stay current with word and phrase changes in your industry or niche and update your list.

4. Use every tense of your words by adding the suffixes -ed, -s, and –ing.

5. Make sure to use your keyword phrases on your website, in a sentence ending in a period. Just listing words on a page doesn't work.

CASE STUDY: Three questions for David Bascom, President of SEO.com

1. *Dave, you spend a lot of time looking at business websites. In your opinion, do businesses pay enough attention to their keyword strategy?*

   No, most businesses don't put enough thought into choosing the right keywords. Keywords are such an important part of marketing a business online because that is how people find you. If you are not targeting the keywords that your potential customers are searching for, you could be missing out on a lot of business. There are many online tools that allow website owners to see how often their selected keywords are searched. This helps people choose keywords with the potential to send you the most possible traffic.

2. *Should people spend time getting links to and from their website to other, similar sites?*

   It's definitely worth the time to work on developing links to your website. Websites with a lot of high quality links are generally viewed by the search engines as being better resources than sites with fewer links. There are many different ways to get links including web directories, press releases, articles, product reviews, testimonials, membership in associations, news stories, and social media. Many of the best links happen naturally when you create useful content or resources on your website for others to link to.

3. *What's one tip you would give anyone who wants to get started optimizing their website for search engines?*

   Remember that even though you're optimizing for the search engines, you're building your website for real, live human beings who will be the ones buying your products. If your site is focused on a specific niche and offers fabulous content, search engine optimization will be a much easier process.

For additional information: SEO.com has helped hundreds of companies grow their businesses through improved search engine visibility. Check out www.SEO.com. They also offer tips, resources, and tools for search engine optimization.

Making the Most of Your Keywords

The term search engine optimization (SEO) can seem intimidating, but really, all it means is that you're using the correct keywords to their utmost potential. When I ask small business CEOs and Presidents about SEO, they often say, "I don't know, but my webmaster does." This is a troubling answer—unless their webmaster is in frequent contact with them, these CEOs have abdicated responsibility for their website. This is unthinkable in an age where so much business is done online. If you work hand in glove with your webmaster and know what he's doing, that's ideal. You don't need to become a web developer, but you should know enough about your website to help make it as accessible and popular as possible.

Five Tips for Optimizing Your Website

You and your webmaster need to focus on these five items when working on optimizing your site for keywords."

- **Page names**—This is the file name given to each page. Try to put your keywords in the page names. Remember, once you create the names for your domain and other pages, do not change them when you redesign your site or you run the risk of going down in organic rankings.
- **Page headings**—These are the designated text headlines on the page that the spider of a search engine can find.
- **Alternate text (Alt Text)**—This is text that refers to images or other things that search engine spiders can't see. The text is put there as an alternate to the image. This means that when the spider comes to an image on your website, your webmaster has put text there to

"describe" the image for the spider. This is also used by engines to support accessibility.

- **Body copy**—This is the copy that everyone can read, including spiders. Obviously, you want your keywords here.
- **Site map**—This is used by both the spider and readers to see what's on the site. Don't forget to create one.

> **Alert!**
>
> Spotlight your important pages: One of the key things you need to do when working with your webmaster is determine the most important pages on your site and make sure they are optimized for your keywords, so that these are the pages people are linked to from search engines. Then, you can drill down and add keywords to all your other pages as you go forward.

Keyword Density

Many SEO professionals disagree about the percentage of keyword density you should have on your pages. Some say don't have a keyword density higher than 1 percent. (For example, if you have 250 words, don't repeat your keyword or phrase more than two or three times.) Others say there is no hard and fast rule. Ultimately, you have to look at what your competitors do and make some common sense decisions.

You have to find a balance between making sure you are including your keywords and supplying readable information. You don't want to overdo it and turn people off, but you also don't want to miss an opportunity to rise in the search engine rankings by having more hits on a particular keyword. Write the copy as you naturally would, then see where you can find places for the keyword. And be sure to ask someone to review it for you.

Developing a PPC Ad Strategy

The key to a smart advertising campaign is a solid strategy. Like everything else in business (and life), it helps if you know what you want to accomplish and why before you jump in. PPC campaigns can seem like mysterious business, but they are just like everything else—you want to start by creating a strategy that fits your needs and your budget. It's perfectly acceptable not to spend a fortune on advertising, but it's not advisable to do it without a strategy.

Developing Your Strategy and Testing Your Ads

To develop a strategy for a PPC campaign, you'll need to ask yourself:

• What do I want to achieve with this campaign?

This is the single most important question to ask yourself. Just like with an overall plan, "If you don't know where you're going, any road will take you there." It's not enough to want more customers—that's a given, or you wouldn't be advertising. You need to be very specific about your goal. Do you want to sign up more readers to your newsletter? Do you want to sell a product that has an upsell to a more expensive product? Whatever the goal, it will determine how you frame your ad and where you direct your links.

• What is my budget?

If you are running an ongoing campaign like Google AdWords, the advertising program on the world's most popular search engine, you are able to set a budget so that you don't blow everything in one day. Setting an overall budget helps you decide how to divide up your budget so that you can accomplish everything you need. If you are spending one-third of your budget on AdWords and one-third on ads in newsletters, you know how much you can spend on each and still have enough left over to do special promotions.

Pay-per-click payments: The way that most PPC advertising works is you pay a certain amount per click you receive to your website, and you can set a limit on what you pay per day. For instance, you could pay ten cents per click and set a limit of ten dollars per day. You're not charged when your ad is displayed, only when someone clicks on it.

- ## Which niche is the focus of this campaign?

You can easily answer that question if you only have one niche, but chances are, you will be promoting to more than one, and you need to make sure you don't mix up your targets. You don't want your luxury soap advertisement running on search results for laundry detergent, for example.

- ## Which keywords will be optimized for each ad?

Make sure to decide before hand which keywords you are testing and put only those in your ad. If you have several different keywords, create one ad for each that uses only those specific keywords.

- ## How long will my campaign last?

Figure out how long you want your test to run and stick to it. You can let your campaigns run longer after you've tested them and know they generate income. Don't plan to run something for any length of time without testing first.

Your PPC campaign

Once you have a list of keywords and a strategy that you've proven successful, you will be able to implement your PPC campaign. Don't feel you have to run a big campaign on day one, but instead go slowly and evaluate what you are doing. Once you decide to do a PPC campaign, there are several you can try. Yahoo and MSN have them. For our purposes, I will concentrate on Google's PPC offer, AdWords. Google has lots of help and training for AdWords; use as much of it as you need before launching a full-scale campaign.

To get started with AdWords you need to sign up, put in a credit card, and follow the instructions to create a campaign. Next, you want to do three things:

1. Determine how much you want to bid on your keywords.

You can determine the top bid by following the link "want to purchase the most clicks possible?" But more important than getting the most clicks possible is controlling your budget. There are many horror stories about people who set up their accounts and didn't put any limits on spending. Make sure you set a daily budget and a maximum cost per click. That way you won't bust your budget.

2. Find the amount of traffic that's estimated for your keywords.

Google has a traffic estimator that you should use to plug in and evaluate your potential traffic. It will show you an estimate of how many clicks you'll get for the words or phrases you have chosen.

3. Do actual searches with your keywords to see what the "search engine results pages" (SERPs) look like.

You don't want any surprises. Check out the sponsored competition and see whether you think they're really a competitor, or if your keywords look to be off-topic. It's a good reality check.

Alert!

Remember to check your bids: Frequently test and check your bids. You don't want to overpay, and you want to be on the lookout for click fraud. If you don't look at your results on a continuous basis, you won't spot problems and valuable search time will be lost.

Next, you need to determine the key messages for your ad so you can test them. For a Google AdWords campaign, you are testing the headline, the short description, the display URL and the destination URL.

AdWords allows A/B testing, which means that you can test two variations of the ad concurrently. Google will rotate them for you. When doing A/B testing, make sure the messages are different enough to provide information. Also, be sure to update ads if the keywords and acronyms of your industry changes.

Using your ad budget wisely: Don't feel you have to run a PPC ad to have online success—you can still appear in the organic search results without buying anything. You need to make sure a PPC ad integrates with everything else you are doing. Determine if the money could be spent elsewhere to greater effect before you spend it.

QUICK Tip

Search Engines to Try: Local Search. Use local search when appropriate. Local search gives specific results to targeted people in a certain area, kind of like an online Yellow Pages. If you run a business that only operates in a certain geographic area, don't forget to consider local search. Make sure your keywords contain the city, street, and any other pertinent information so that you can be found. Google Maps is an example of a local search engine, as is local.yahoo.com.

Shopping Search Engines. With the interest in customer opinions and reviews, search engines specifically for shopping are becoming more important. The top four independent shopping engines in 2007 were Bizrate, Shopping.com, Shopzilla and NexTag. According to Hitwise, an online competitive intelligence service, these four together had 61 percent of the shopping search engine market. Look into placing product pages here if it's appropriate.

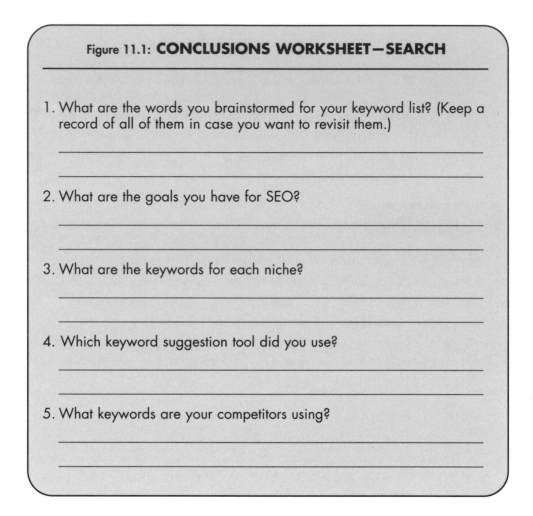

Figure 11.1: **CONCLUSIONS WORKSHEET—SEARCH**

1. What are the words you brainstormed for your keyword list? (Keep a record of all of them in case you want to revisit them.)

2. What are the goals you have for SEO?

3. What are the keywords for each niche?

4. Which keyword suggestion tool did you use?

5. What keywords are your competitors using?

Chapter 12

Step 5. Content

Good communication is as stimulating as black coffee and just as hard to sleep after.
— Anne Morrow Lindbergh

- ◗ **Your Content Today**
- ◗ **Writing for the Web**
- ◗ **Six Rules of Persuasion**
- ◗ **Landing Pages**
- ◗ **Minisites and Sales Letters**

Good online content is the key to getting and keeping loyal customers. You should have two goals for all your content—to sell and to educate. If you fulfill both of these, your customers will return to your website often to learn and buy.

Your Content Today

To start evaluating your content, take a big picture look at what you're trying to accomplish with your site and determine the level of quality vs. quantity. Your online goal is always to make it easy for customers to buy from you, and your content is very important in accomplishing that. Here are some things you should do to ensure value:

1. Have different types of content for each type of learner so that everyone finds the information they need in the format they respond to (i.e., audio, video). Make sure to label it as such to let the visitor know what kind of content it is before downloading.
   Example: podcasts with experts on the topic; marketing video to explain product benefits; recorded webinars of sales presentations; audio or video testimonials.
2. Have extra content ready to help facilitate an impulse buy.
   Example: downloadable pricing sheets; testimonials; tech specs; photos of the product from a variety of angles.
3. Have information for buyers at every stage of the process so that they don't have to leave your site to find the information they need to make a buying decision.
   Example: create information sheets for beginning, intermediate, and experienced buyers of your product or service. No one will be offended if you give them the choice to be treated like a newbie if they are a newbie, and it will make your experienced buyers feel knowledgeable.
4. Provide comparison charts between your products and the competition.
   Example: special features; pricing; tech specs.
5. Provide a forum where customers can talk to one another.
   Example: create a message board and encourage users to post help tips, show how they use the product, etc.

6. Provide a place for customer ratings and opinions.

   Example: create a page for feedback where users tell you what they like and don't like. Don't silence contrarians.

Writing for the Web

When writing your online content, you need to think about how the reader will scan it. People reading websites scan: they jump around quickly looking at the headings, subheads, and captions to determine if they are interested.

Figure 12.1: **ONLINE CONTENT DOS AND DON'TS**

Dos	Don'ts
Do put the most important information first.	Don't make your type too small. Not everyone can see as well as you can.
Do use bulleted lists.	Don't use different colors of text on the page. You can use bold for emphasis, but too many colors or embellishments will look cluttered and hard to read.
Do use descriptive words for links whenever possible instead of just "click here."	Don't change typeface more than once or twice on a page.
Do clearly state the problem you solve with your product or service and use that copy in subheads.	Don't forget to use lots of white space. Scanning requires the eye to jump from place to place. If it's all solid text, scanning is hard and people won't read it.
Do make sure you break up long paragraphs with subheads.	Don't eliminate important information—write it in bite-sized pieces so that the reader is not overwhelmed.
Do keep your margins wide.	

Six Rules of Persuasion

As mentioned, content should both sell and educate, and part of selling is persuading the buyer that they have found the product that suits them best. In his classic book, *Influence*, psychology professor Robert B. Cialdini outlines the six key ways people are persuaded. He uncovered these principles by conducting experiments at the college where he teaches and by talking to the people who are in the business of persuasion—salespeople, fund raisers, advertisers, etc.

He came away with six principles that are accepted truths today. You'll recognize all of them—direct mail and web marketers have applied these rules to great effect. See how you can apply them to your product or service.

1. **Reciprocation**—We try to pay someone back for something they have given us.

   How this applies to your online marketing—This one is very common. Have you ever given your email address in exchange for an e-book or sample? You've reciprocated, and likely felt comfortable doing so—you've gotten something you wanted. This is a common web transaction and one you make offline everyday.

2. **Commitment and consistency**—Once we make a decision, we try to line up our beliefs and actions to be consistent with that decision.

   How this applies to your online marketing—People are uncomfortable if they act in a way that is not consistent with their beliefs. If you can point out how people are inconsistent, they will change their behavior. For example, watch any life insurance commercial on TV—they make the case that, if you love your family so much, prove it by taking care of them after you're gone.

3. **Social Proof**—When deciding how to act in a situation we follow what we see other people doing. You've heard the taunt, "Monkey see, monkey do."

   How this applies to your online marketing—This principle explains why testimonials are placed in abundance with any offer. People want to be reassured that they are not the only ones making a decision. They want to know that others have already made it and are happy.

4. **Liking**—People associate with people they like and want to say yes to their requests. They want to be liked in return, so saying yes whenever possible makes them comfortable.

   How this applies to your online marketing—Author Tim Sanders wrote about this extensively in his book, *The Likeability Factor*. I'm sure this is something you know intuitively. You want to do business with people you like, so you need to be likeable. This ties into the power of social networking that allows you to interact with a wider circle of "friends."

5. **Authority**—People have a tendency to comply when they are asked to do something by someone they believe has authority.

   How this applies to your online marketing—This is why you see gurus on the Web endorsing other gurus. They know that if you believe a person to hold a high rank, you're more likely to feel good about doing what they ask or using the product they endorse.

6. **Scarcity**—People are prone to want things they think are hard to get.
   How this applies to your online marketing—This principle made the iPhone a big story in 2007. People camped out at retail stores overnight, hoping to snare one of the available units. The fact that they did not sell out was irrelevant. There was no way to know upfront whether there would be enough to go around. People were shown on the news triumphantly holding up their iPhones. This provides the buyer with a memorable experience. That's also why there was a backlash when the price was dropped $200 shortly thereafter. This caused those who believed in the scarcity to feel upset.

   This tactic is also used when marketers put a time limit on sales: "Limited offer, good through June 1." The idea is to make the customer take action instead of procrastinating.

Landing Pages

If you understand their power, landing pages can be your marketing success secret. Landing pages are the place your customer is taken after they click on the link to your site in an advertisement. They are companion pages to your advertisements, but they're also valuable little tools that can make or break your advertising success. Landing pages are basically targeted home pages for a specific offer. In 2008, no one should be sent to a home page from an ad of any kind. It's too confusing and doesn't really do the job. You want to craft your offer to make sure the customer has everything they need to support an impulse buy. Sending a person to your home page is an ineffective way to present an offer—send them directly to the offer.

Recent studies have shown that landing pages with a few options are better than landing pages with only one option or taking the viewer to a home page with many options. You want to give the reader a specific path to take to end up as a buyer but you don't want to give them only a yes or no choice.

QUICK Tip

Common flaws in landing pages: Marketing Sherpa, publisher of Internet case studies, report in their *Landing Page Handbook* that the common landing page has these flaws:

- Makes people read (90 percent of the population doesn't like reading)
- Forces people to type names, addresses, etc.
- Requires a phone number
- Makes the customer risk spamming by giving their email address
- Has the customer provide a credit card that could be used for fraudulent purposes
- Makes people pay

Every landing page should be a reflection of what you know about your customer and provide what they need to know to make a buying decision. If you are successful with your landing page, you are creating an ad that will take your customer through the process to your shopping cart or desired action. Don't make the mistake of thinking that if your customer wants the product he will jump through hoops. He won't. Make your landing pages compelling, but most of all, make them easy.

Three good reasons to use a landing page:
1. Depending on how you create web pages, it's very inexpensive.
2. The content is flexible—you don't have to conform to the style of your website, so you can tailor each landing page to your specific needs for the product at hand.
3. You should be able to revise it quickly and test until you are satisfied.

The Rules of Creating Powerful Landing Pages

1. Determine your one customer goal

Determine the final action you want your visitor to take and make that the goal of the page. When you achieve this result, you can deem your landing page campaign a success.

You may have a list of things you want to accomplish and think the landing page might be a good place to try everything at once—it's not. Too much content on a landing page can be confusing to your visitor. If your goal is to get their email address, make sure you provide an incentive and make it the centerpiece of your page. Typically, you might offer a free e-book or a white paper in exchange for their email address. Be clear about what you want. If you're not clear, you can bet your reader will leave without taking action.

2. Make it consistent with the ad

Whether the link to the landing page was on a Google pop-up ad or a full color magazine page, make sure that the ad and page go together to create a cohesive message with matching graphics. To test this, simulate what the visitor will do—read your ad and then click to your landing page. If your message is inconsistent, the path to your goal will be lost; the customer might think the link took them to the wrong place. Consistency will ensure that the customer knows they've found what they were looking for.

3. Present a professional design

Your landing page must equal the quality of your website. The fact that your landing page functions as a single ad doesn't mean that visitors won't expect a well-designed page with graphics. This doesn't have to be expensive, just well-thought-out.

4. Don't include extraneous links

Carefully lay out the path you want your visitors to take. Think about it like a visit to a museum. In a museum, the direction and place the visitor should walk is carefully delineated so that they get the maximum viewing effect. It also keeps the line moving. Your landing page should do the same. Decide the path you want them to take and narrow your text and links to follow that path. Don't throw everything on the page in the hope that you will hit on something that interests them. It's not a scavenger hunt.

5. Call for action

You know that anyone who visits your landing page is interested in your product or services, since they had to click on a link to get there. Make sure the visitor knows what she needs to do next. If she is interested, you want to make it clear that she should call, type in her email address, or take some other pre-determined action. This is the point at which she will be the most motivated to act on her interest in your company. Don't miss this opportunity.

6. Track your results

To determine if your campaign is cost-effective, you'll want to measure your results. These are the two most important statistics to track:

a. *Conversion rate (%):*
   The easiest measurement to take is your conversion rate. It is the number of visitors who made a purchase divided by the number of visitors to your landing page.

b. Marketing Cost per Sale ($):

This is the cost of your landing page divided by the number of sales you attribute to the landing page. This will let you determine if your landing page campaign is a good investment.

In terms of refining your campaign, you can try split A/B testing and other tests, but the most important thing to remember is that if you start with a good solid campaign plan, you will have a much higher success rate.

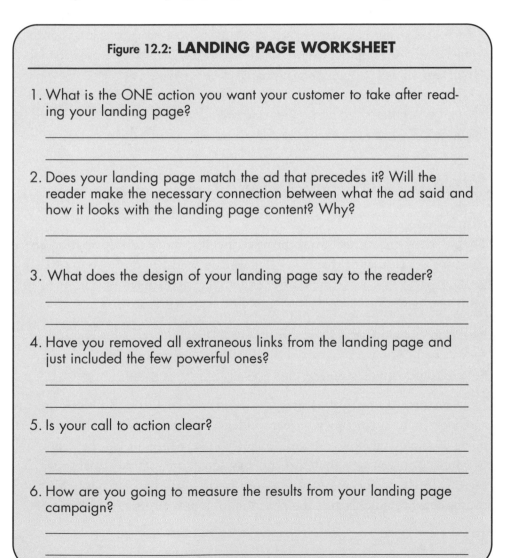

Figure 12.2: **LANDING PAGE WORKSHEET**

1. What is the ONE action you want your customer to take after reading your landing page?

2. Does your landing page match the ad that precedes it? Will the reader make the necessary connection between what the ad said and how it looks with the landing page content? Why?

3. What does the design of your landing page say to the reader?

4. Have you removed all extraneous links from the landing page and just included the few powerful ones?

5. Is your call to action clear?

6. How are you going to measure the results from your landing page campaign?

A Word on Copyright

There has been a lot of controversy regarding the abuse of copyrights on the Web. The simple way to approach a very complex topic—protect your material with a copyright and don't violate others' copyrights.

For example, don't use copyrighted photos to sell your products unless you buy the rights. Don't appropriate published articles you don't have permission for, and keep an eye out to make sure your employees understand what a copyright is and what material they can safely use. If you have any doubt about something you're thinking about posting, don't use it.

Minisites and Sales Letters

Minisites

The purpose of a minisite is to provide specific, targeted information about one topic. It is smaller than a regular website and has more content than a landing page. It is used most effectively when you have one item to sell. Minisites can:

- sell one product or service effectively and keep the reader focused
- pick and optimize one or two keywords successfully
- be updated quickly and often

A fun viral example of a minisite was created by CareerBuilder.com. You can view it at http://www.careerbuilder.com/age-o-matic/. This site purports to show you how you will look if you stay in your "soul-sucking" job too long. You can see that the site has some interactive capabilities, but focuses solely on the message that you need to find a better job. Minisites can be used to quickly test the potential of a new product or offering.

Sales Letters

I'm sure you've all seen the very popular online sales letters that information marketers and others use. They follow the direct mail formula of an emotion grabbing headline followed by lots of testimonials and supporting evidence. Their purpose is to provide enough information to convince the customer to buy in one sitting. The difference between a minisite and a sales letter is that a minisite can have more than one page, whereas a sales letter is one long web page. An example of a successful sales letter from great copywriter Lorrie Morgan-Ferrero is online at http://www.red-hot-copy.com/.

If done correctly, sales letters work—like any good offer, the key is matching the right product with the right sales and advertising tactics. Sales letters should be very focused on one product and confined to one long web page. It has been shown that longer letters work better than having users click to other pages. Each click eliminates a group of readers.

QUICK Tip

Ten Characteristics of Good Sales Letters
1. Use an emotional headline.
2. Offer a benefit immediately and have a list of benefits throughout.
3. Include real-life testimonials of satisfied users of the product or service.
4. Repeat information as needed.
5. Have a clear call to action.
6. Write personalized copy that focuses on your specific audience.
7. Make the offer time-limited.
8. Present an honest assessment—too many of these have overhyped copy that promises "the world's greatest widget!"
9. Tell a story the person can relate to with some of the power words we discussed in the Content section.
10. Show proof in the form of statistics or other numbers to back up your claim.

Figure 12.3: **CONCLUSIONS WORKSHEET—CONTENT**

1. Do you have adequate information for each of your four content "must-haves?" (About Us, Support and contact, Help and FAQs, Press Room)

_____

_____

2. Have you analyzed your content to ensure that you don't make the three beginner's mistakes? What did you find?

_____

_____

3. Did you fill out the Landing Page Worksheet? Are you satisfied with it?

_____

_____

4. Will you use a sales letter? Did you create the content?

_____

_____

Chapter 13

Step 6. Tactics—Social Media

Be careful what you pretend to be because you are what you pretend to be.

—Kurt Vonnegut

- Blogging and Microblogging
- Videos and Podcasting
- Social Networks
- Your Own Online Community
- Wikis
- Social Bookmarking and Tagging
- Customer Reviews and Ratings

As we have discussed, it is important to determine which social media tactics are right for your business, but here are a few that you should definitely explore. After you read about them, you can decide which ones fit into your 7 Step Action Plan.

Alert!

One at a time: Don't try to do everything at once. Each social media tactic requires careful thought and integration into your overall strategy. Pick the ones that you think will have immediate impact and add news ones as they fit into your plan and your schedule.

Remember that all the tactics we look at will support and strengthen each other—you want to build them into a system that produces interest in your products and services. For example, unless you have a huge following, you will probably not make money just by starting a blog. But, if you sell products from your blog or develop leads for your products, your blog has done its job. You should consider each tactic as part of a working system that creates a steady stream of interested customers.

Blogging and Microblogging

With all the hype surrounding blogging, it may seem like a complex topic, but don't worry—there are really only two important things to know: (1) how a blog will benefit and grow your business; and (2) how it provides marketing benefits that are different from your company website so you can get the most from each channel.

 **A blog history:** The word "blog" is short for the phrase "web log." Web logs started as online diaries that people used to post their daily thoughts. Obviously, the tactic has exploded over the last few years and millions of people now have blogs. In August 2007, Technorati.com (a blog index) reported tracking 101.3 million blogs. The majority of these are personal and probably only read by one or two people, but lots of businesses have found them invaluable for their online marketing.

Seven Business Benefits of a Blog

1. It reinforces the idea that you are an expert in your field.
2. It helps pull a community of like-minded people together.
3. You get useful feedback from people who have bought or might buy your product.
4. It increases the likelihood that the media can find you and write about your products. ZDNet Research reports that 67 percent of journalists use blogs as sources and that 35 percent have their own blogs.
5. It helps develop the brand story so that people can tell others about you and generate further leads.
6. The content is always fresh, so your business demonstrates that you are active and responsive.
7. It generates traffic to your website and any other links you include on your blog.

You can see there's a great deal of benefit. But how does a blog differ from a website?

A blog benefits you in ways your website can't:

- It's interactive—readers can comment and you can establish a dialogue with your customers. That means it's two-way conversation, which is critical in today's market.
- It's immediate—content is published instantly and search engines find it quickly.
- Its inherent structure allows you to archive content for interested readers to search.
- You can create an RSS feed of your blog to ensure that whoever wants to stay updated can get your information easily.
- You have increased exposure to search engines, which love the constantly changing content.
- You don't have to be a "techie" to create a blog. The tools are readily available. Two good blogging platforms are www.typepad.com and www.wordpress.com. If you're new to the whole idea of blogging, I recommend a great resource list put together by blogger Darren Rowse at Problogger.com You'll find the resources at http://www.problogger.net/archives/2006/04/15/blog-tools/.
- You can comment on other people's blogs and get more exposure for your brand, sending more traffic back to your site.

QUICK Tip

Get your feet wet: If you are new to blogging you can begin a blog using one of the standard services without making it public. This means that no one will see it until you are ready. Try it out for two weeks and see if you want to continue with the content you have and the posting schedule you have established.

Blog Myths

Some of my clients have told me that they were afraid to start a blog. Why do blogs inspire fear? Perhaps some of these myths have run through your mind:

• You need to be considered cool to write a blog.

Unless your business is built around a celebrity, readers are just hungry for solid information. You can gain a following by delivering great tips and new ideas.

• You'll run out of things to write about.

Like anything else, your interest will wax and wane depending on the topic your blog is covering. Ask your marketing and sales teams to volunteer topics that they are dealing with, and talk to customer service about the topic of the calls each week. Or you can feature an expert guest blogger on a hot topic to spice things up. Also, remember to create an editorial calendar like any good publisher and plan ahead. That way you've planned far enough ahead to ease your anxiety.

• You'll be criticized and unable to withstand the onslaught of negative comments.

There's always a risk of being criticized, but if you follow common sense business rules, you should be engaging in debates about business topics, not personal attacks. If things do get out of hand, use your blog tools to block the people trying to hijack the debate from participating.

• It will take too much of your time.

Don't accept that idea at face value. You need to take a look at the big picture of your business. Ask yourself what you're trying to accomplish and what marketing channels you are using, then evaluate the return for each of those marketing channels. If you're continuing to do a newsletter without much return, perhaps you should consider a blog. If you're spending too much on pay-per-click advertising without a return, maybe writing a blog and publishing an e-newsletter would be better. How you spend your time should be determined by what channels give you the best return.

QUICK Tip

Before you start your blog ask yourself these questions:

- What do I want to accomplish?
- Who is my target audience?
- Will my blog be personal or corporate in tone?
- Will I write the blog alone or with a group or guests?
- How often will I post?
- What kinds of media can I use—e.g., podcasts, photos, video?

Once you are clear about why you are starting a blog, you'll need a title and a tagline. They let visitors know what your blog is about when they reach your page.

Finding an Audience

Once you've come up with the plan for your blog, you'll want to encourage an audience to find it. People can find your blog in several ways: search engines, blog directories, another blog or link, your website, a personal referral, a Google ad campaign, a social networking site, etc.

The first thing you want to do is burn a feed on Feedburner.com and register with blog directories like Technorati.com and the hundreds of other blog directories out there. In addition, you'll want to make sure you tag your blog posts with your keywords. Just creating a blog isn't enough: You need to guide search engines and directories to find you.

Alert!

Work smarter: One easy way to sign up for several blogs at one time is on Robin Good's handy list of RSS site submission sites at http://www.masternewmedia.org/rss/top55/.

Here are some quick ways to help your blog be found:

1. Put a link from your website to your blog and visa versa.
2. Make sure that your blog address is in your signature file so that people who interact with you online know where to find your blog.
3. Make sure to put your blog address in your newsletter, on your business card, and on any other printed matter you distribute.
4. Comment on other blogs that have audiences similar to yours; your comments will link back to you.

QUICK Tip

Don't forget microblogging: Twitter and Pownce are two tools that have evolved with the popularity of blogging. These tools, often called "nanoblogs " or "microblogs" are like instant messages for bloggers. They allow you to keep in constant touch with your friends, family, and colleagues. They can remain apprised of what you are doing at any given moment. From a business perspective, it's too early to tell how valuable these services will be. The only limit is 140 characters per message. If you are working on something that requires you to be in touch with a vendor or colleague on a moment by moment basis, this could be handy. Messages run the gamut from deadly dull to interesting. www.Twitter.com has an API (application programming interface), which means that developers can create custom applications for it. www.Pownce.com is available on Facebook, so that might spur its growth. You can also share documents and other files on Pownce, so it may prove more useful as a business tool. At this time, its marketing potential has not been exploited. As well-known blogger Robert Scoble wrote in September 2007 in his *Fast Company* column "The Next Email: Why Twitter will change the way business communicates (again)," "If we revisit this conversation again in three years, I suspect that we'll have found all sorts of little uses for these services, and they'll simply become what email is today: something we must do to participate in the heartbeat of business."

Videos and Podcasting

The growth of broadband has made it possible for users to watch videos and listen to audio on their computers. Using inexpensive video cameras, podcasting tools, and digital cameras, users are able to create and share their amateur creations with the entire world. YouTube videos shoot around the Web and photos and audio can be found on your favorite search engine instantly. Companies like NetFlix provide customers with the ability to order and watch a movie or TV episode on their PCs almost instantly. It's now a world of twenty-four-hour entertainment, on demand and ready when you are.

A study by the Online Publishers Association released in August 2007 found that the main use of the Internet is moving from communications to content. This is a very significant finding. People are moving such traditionally offline activities as newspaper reading and checking TV listings to the Internet. This means that although people send more emails than ever, their content consumption is rising even faster.

Five Major Benefits of Using Audio and Visual Content

1. Your customers expect it. They want to have multimedia choices and those who don't offer them seem out of touch.
2. Customers can listen or watch whenever they want—they are in control.
3. Users only view them if they want to, so you automatically have an interested audience who wants to hear your message.
4. The cost to create and play multimedia is inexpensive.
5. People from around the world can access your message. You are not limited by geography.

Videos

Do an evaluation of your site content and find a place to include some video. You can do a brief interview with your customers, topic experts, or internal staff—make it short, make it useful, and just make sure you have some video content on your site. And to make sure your videos are found you need to treat them just like you would a blog. Remember to create a video whenever you add or expand a topic; create an RSS feed for it so that updates can be easily received by customers; and register them in search engine directories that specifically index videos so they can easily be found.

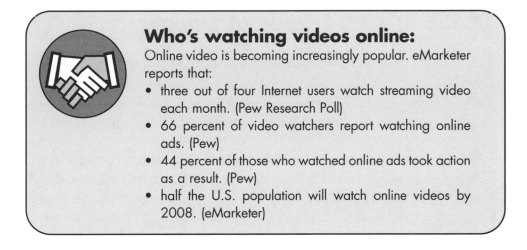

Who's watching videos online:

Online video is becoming increasingly popular. eMarketer reports that:

- three out of four Internet users watch streaming video each month. (Pew Research Poll)
- 66 percent of video watchers report watching online ads. (Pew)
- 44 percent of those who watched online ads took action as a result. (Pew)
- half the U.S. population will watch online videos by 2008. (eMarketer)

Several of my clients have asked me if they need a professional to create their videos and podcasts. The answer depends on who you are and what you are trying to accomplish. Part of the charm of online videos and podcasts is their "home-made" quality. However, as a businessperson you need to weigh the impact that a less than professional presentation will have.

If you are a small company that has a young consumer audience, it may be fine to produce an internal video about your products and upload it to your website. If you are a larger company with business customers, you need to think about what their expectations are. The key is to approach it creatively. This does not mean you need a big budget to hire an expensive advertising agency, but you do want to be sure the audio and video are clear and well-paced.

You can also ask customers to send in their videos to promote a product or enter a contest. This can make for some fun, engaging content on your website, and it's also a great way to find out what your customers really think of your products. Some advertisers have learned the hard way that their customers do not feel positively towards their products.

CASE STUDY: Stand-out videos

Geico.com, a U.S. insurance company, use videos in their commercials that were made to look like they came from a site like YouTube, but their videos are in commercials that look like sleek, professional commercials. Obviously their budget is large, but what makes them standout is their creativity.

Another video standout is Commoncraft.com. They are a company that creates short videos for clients using paper-based "props" to explain a concept. These videos can be found on YouTube.com at http://www.youtube .com/results?search_query=commoncraft&search=tag. Commoncraft's work has gotten popular because they do exactly what a great web video should do: they are short, to the point, and explain a useful concept. Check them out for an example of online video done right.

Podcasting

Podcasting allows everyone to have a broadcast microphone. Creating podcasts is easy to do and they can be placed on your website, in blogs, newsletters, and any other online channels you create. You can create an RSS feed specifically for your podcasts to make sure customers who want audio will get it.

Several different services are available to help you create podcasts if you don't have an in-house technical person. I use a service called www.AudioAcrobat.com which requires a small monthly subscription fee. Another popular free tool for podcasting is Audacity, which is found at http://audacity.sourceforge.net/

Who listens to podcasts: In 2007, Edison Media Research did a study of podcast listeners. Podcast listeners are:

- 49 percent female; 51 percent male
- Two times more likely than the average person to make over $100,000 per year
- 36 percent more likely to make online purchases

Sound like a group you might be interested in marketing to?

Social Networks

It has often been said that it's not what you know, but who you know. Social networking sites bring people together to communicate in ways unimaginable just a decade ago. For the online marketer, these networks provide a wonderful opportunity to learn what's being said about your products and services. They may also help you network with potential partners and customers. Marketing on social networks will become more prevalent when businesses figure out how to exploit the information they learn about people sharing personal information. They will succeed if they figure out how to fit into the framework of the community and not become another source of "interruption marketing." Only time will tell.

There are established social networking sites that you may want to look at to help you network with colleagues and potential customers. According to comScore, social networking sites drew over eleven million unique monthly visitors in July 2007, which is up 40 percent from the previous July. I think you should take a cautious look at them. If you don't see a clear cut advantage for yourself, don't join just to say you joined.

Let's look at a few of the major social networks.

LinkedIn For Business Professionals

www.LinkedIn.com is a social network that currently hosts over eleven million business people who list their information and hope to find networking contacts and new business. Some people use it to source job applicants and others use it to find new business opportunities. Hitwise reported that in July 2007, 31.3 percent of the traffic came from twenty-five- to thirty-four-year–olds.

Is LinkedIn for you? It may be. Its user base is growing and there is now an upgrade to a paid subscription. Like any social network, you need to put some effort in, in order to get something tangible from it.

QUICK Tip

Three ways to use LinkedIn

1. Use it to speak to people you would not otherwise have access to. Your list of contacts serves as the starting point for you to meet others on their contact lists. You can often reach someone in a specific company or position who you want to know.
2. Use it to show others your expertise by answering questions posted by other users. This gives you visibility and credibility. If your answer is picked as the best of those submitted on the topic, you get an extra boost.
3. See who is hiring to determine what kinds of activity is happening in a particular company or industry.

Some other comparable sites to consider are www.md.sermo.com (for medical professionals),www.Activerain.com (for real estate professionals), and www.AdGabber.com (for advertising professionals).

Facebook for "Friends"

Just for college kids? Not any more. Since June 2006, comScore Media Matrix has reported a 113 percent rise in Facebook visitors over the age of thirty-five. That makes up 41 percent of the sites visitors. People around the world can connect with one another on Facebook and easily join groups of like-minded people they would not have met otherwise.

We are still in the early stages of figuring out what's important for marketers to do on Facebook. It may succeed as a marketing platform in ways that MySpace has not. Unlike MySpace, Facebook decided to open up their network to developers. What that means is developers can create applications for Facebook users to employ. According to the September 2007 issue of *Business 2.0*, in the ten weeks since it was open to developers, there were 2,500 new applications created that triggered 139 million downloads. These applications run the gamut from ways to donate to charities to favorite movie picks.

At this point in time, I think Facebook has demonstrated that it can be useful as a networking tool for business owners, but still has to prove itself as a small business marketing tool. Given all the other tactics available, I wouldn't rush into this one.

MySpace

If you're marketing to Generation Y this could be a good place to expend some effort. It depends on your marketing savvy with this age group. MySpace was launched in 2004 by Tom Anderson and Chris de Wolfe. It was purchased by media mogul Rupert Murdoch in 2005. Currently it has 65 million users who use their MySpace page to put their profiles, photos, blog posts, video, and links online.

Like Facebook, I'm not sure it's the best place for you to concentrate marketing efforts right now. It requires tenacity and a good understanding of the tools and the audience. If you wanted to actually purchase advertising space, it's very expensive, so that's not a good play for small businesses. If you are interested in exploring it, I'd recommend that you start slow and join with the idea that you'll learn about it and make "friends." Once you feel comfortable that you understand the space, you can go further with marketing efforts that fit.

Advertising on Social Networks

If you want to try advertising on social networks and have a limited budget, I would put this on the bottom of the list for further exploration. However, here are some things to consider when you feel you have done enough research about the audience and its etiquette to appeal to them and find a strategy that's profitable for you:

1. **Ads.** Buy ads from Google AdWords or an ad network that works with Facebook like Lookery.com.

2. **Sponsorship.** Sponsoring an application that is pertinent to your audience is a way to get applications working for you. You'll want to look at sites like Appaholic.com to see what's popular.

3. **Facebook Marketplace.** These are like classifieds where people buy and sell everything from fine art to concert tickets. You could place an ad for your product here.

Your Own Online Community

Creating your own online community is a great way to harness the enthusiasm and the collective intelligence of your customers. You will hear conflicting advice about whether it pays to create your own community. Some people say you should seek out an already formed community and find your audience within it. Others say it pays to create a group specifically devoted to your products. I think both are worth doing; there is no reason to exclude either course. (You'll find more about collaborating with customers in Chapter 18: Collaboration with Colleagues and Customers.)

QUICK Tip

Four Benefits to Starting Your Own Online Community

1. You can learn how your customers express themselves, giving you a chance to find new keywords and product ideas.
2. You can use the information to write web copy and tutorials.
3. It creates a mailing list of people who want to hear your product messages.
4. You can learn what misperceptions there are about your products and correct them.

If you think an online community would work for you, here are some questions you need to think about before you get started:

1. Are you willing to listen to your members? Their feedback is likely to be both good and bad. An online community will grow if members are respected for comments that are not always positive, although always civil.

2. What will the graphical look of the site be and who will create it? You'll want to brand your community with your graphics if it is company-related. It should look like an extension of your website in tone and substance. Don't represent your company with a sloppy online presentation. If your community is targeted at only one segment of your audience, make sure to brand it to appeal to that segment.

3. How will you recruit new members and alert interested potential members? You need to think about how you will let your audience know that you have established a community and that you want them to join.

4. What will the forum discussion topics be? You'll want to create content new members can engage in. Think about adding content to your forums before you open it up to visitors. You want to have something for them to react to and generate some excitement. Plan to use polls, games, and other interactive features that will keep members coming back.

5. How will you use the feedback about your products? One of the goals of an online community is to get feedback from your customers. Make sure management intends to listen to it and respond. If not, your community will be disappointed and leave. This is the opposite effect you want it to have, so prepare management beforehand. If you have a new product, feature, or service you are going to launch, solicit feedback from your community members. You want them to feel like insiders whenever possible.

6. Who in-house will be responsible for moderating the community? Supporting an online community is a big undertaking. Make sure someone is assigned to monitor it and keep the action going. If it languishes, it will appear as though your company doesn't value its members. Special content will be needed, as well as repurposed content from your blogs and website. Hire an outside group to help create content if need be. Use a variety of multimedia formats to keep visitors engaged. Also, solicit multimedia like video and podcasts from members.

7. Will the group be private or public? If it's public, anyone can join. If it's private, you need an invitation. Decide if you want a closed group

that can only join by invitation. This would be appropriate for small advisory groups. If you want to reach a large, diverse audience, make it public.

8. How will you make it easy for members to interact with each other as well as the community leader? Members should have the ability to create their own blogs and share pictures.

CASE STUDY: Two good, free tools to help you start or join communities

Ning

www.Ning.com was founded by Marc Andreessen and Gina Bianchini in 2005. It lets you set up your own online community and has all the bells and whistles you need, like being able to post photos and add comments to forums. In October 2007 there were one hundred thousand different social networks set up on Ning. It's easy to create a network and if you are prepared to put the effort into making it interesting for your members, it can be a very worthwhile investment of your time.

Squidoo

www.Squidoo.com is a different kind of online community. Started by Seth Godin in 2005, it is made up of a network of users who set up topic pages called lenses. As a "lensmaster" you can share your expertise and information about your company or any topic you are passionate about. You need to join the community to build a lens and it's incredibly easy.

A lens is a hybrid—it can function like a blog where you post and recommend things, and you can also join groups of like-minded lens makers. It's free, you can easily support a charity, and it's spidered by search engines. You should give this one a try.

Wikis

Wikis are databases of collaborative information. The most well known wiki is Wikipedia.com, an encyclopedia edited by millions of readers around the world. It is a repository of information that can be added to, but not erased. This is an important distinction. Once something is accepted, there is a record of it. When someone revises it, the old record remains. That way, if there is some dispute about the content, the old information is available for review.

The key thing to know about wikis is that any size company can use them. You don't have to be a huge corporation with specialized information. To understand how they might help your business, let's look at how they can be used. Your employees gather new information each day. If these employees had a place to update project information, it would be easier for everyone to keep abreast of changes.

For example, Sony created a Wiki for their PlayStation team. As new developments occur, anyone on the team can log in and see what's happening. This means that the legal department and the marketing people can communicate. There are several online tools you can use to create a wiki. Some easy ones to try are www.PBWiki.com and www.EditMe.com.

Social Bookmarking and Tagging

What is bookmarking? Bookmarks are created when someone using a browser marks a favorite web page (known as "Favorites" in Internet Explorer) to capture the location of a page to which they want to return. It's just like a bookmark you put in a physical book.

Social bookmarking allows readers to sign up and bookmark and publicly tag (keyword) information and share it in a searchable way. Generally, the information can be searched by category, keyword, person, or popularity. This helps make it more "findable." (This process of groups categorizing information is known as a "folksonomy.") There is a collective web of information on these bookmarking sites that allows people to make connections with others who have similar interests.

The first well-known social bookmarking site was www.del.icio.us, founded in 2003 (now owned by Yahoo). Next, in 2004, came Digg.com, which allowed users to vote on the content they found most interesting.

Readers submit stories they find interesting and users vote on their importance.

Next came StumbleUpon.com (acquired by eBay in May 2007). It is a web browser plug-in that allows users to find web pages, photos, videos, and news articles, much like you do with any web browser. The key benefit is that it lets you rate and share them with others.

The Benefits of Social Bookmarking

The value of social bookmarking is twofold:

1. Connect with others

You can organize and share information that you find valuable. This helps you connect with people who can provide additional information about topics you find interesting.

2. Drive traffic

You can drive traffic to your site from people who find your information and are interested in finding out more about your products or services.

You need to test your efforts on these tools to determine whether: (1) the traffic you receive translates into revenue; and (2) the contacts and information are valuable. Analyze what happens. I want you to know about how to use these tools, but you should also temper your enthusiasm for them as a traffic tool until you are sure they work for you.

Customer Reviews and Ratings

On customer review sites, "Users treat brands like contestants on *American Idol*." That apt description was written by Joan Voight in a July 2007 column on Brandweek.com. It's true. Users no longer worship at the altar of "The Brand." Products are picked apart, scoffed at, and treated to a daily round of claps and jeers. But the possibility of a negative review doesn't mean you can forget about hosting customer reviews and ratings. Bazaarvoice.com, a company that hosts online product reviews and ratings for companies, says that, "76 percent of US shoppers consider it important to read customer reviews before making a purchase."

Customers will find reviews: If you don't have customer reviews on your site, people will look elsewhere for confirmation before buying your product. There are sites like www.ConsumerSearch.com and www.epinions.com where users independently voice their opinions.

Whether you host reviews on your own site, or they appear on an independent site, you can't escape the scrutiny. What you need to decide is whether it is worth it to you to host your own reviews. In May 2007, a Marketing Sherpa study found that 58 percent of those surveyed said they "strongly prefer" sites with reviews.

One way to determine if there is pent-up demand for this feature is to research how often your products are being written about and what's being said. If you have a lot of discussion but you aren't ready to host reviews, try a blog, where people can comment. You can also survey your customers to see whether they want it. It's your call as to what you do—just don't ignore it.

CASE STUDY: Three questions for Bob Morse, President, Morse Associates, and Martin Middlewood, President, Frontline Strategies Inc.

1. With all the great social media tools out there, are case studies still relevant? (Here our definition of case study refers to a study of a business problem and why it succeeded or failed.)

The customer voice brings credibility to sales and marketing efforts. They help prospects imagine using a product or service to solve their problem.

Web 2.0 tools provide a new opportunity to enhance customer reference programs. Customers or vendors can set up either external or internal blogs or wikis to track the deployment and adoption of new technologies within organizations. They can increase their interactions and at the same time explain how they solved any problems they encountered.

2. Are there social media tactics that apply to case studies?

Developing a case study release that has tags and keywords incorporated into it, then distributing it through the proper media channels is a powerful social media tool for case study marketing. So are links in company blogs pointing to case studies. Tagging, wikis, and RSS feeds also show promise. Vendors might consider wikis that combine all their customers' experiences with a particular technology to provide a more balanced view of it. Vendors might tag their case studies on their sites to improve searching accuracy. They might also add RSS feeds to their case study pages so customers searching for solutions know when new information is available.

3. What is the one tip you would give anyone planning to develop and use case studies to sell their products?

If something doesn't meet your customers' expectations, you can bet there's a dialogue somewhere about it. So a vendor's choice is to participate or not. Those companies that manage their customers' experience from beginning to end and use Web 2.0 tools will gain respect, because they will provide information that is more credible. Case studies coming out of these experiences will be gold nuggets. So companies should collect, refine, and show them off widely. Then simply repeat the process.

Additional Resources: Check out their blog at www.casestudy411.com.

Figure 13.1: CONCLUSIONS WORKSHEET—SOCIAL MEDIA TACTICS

1. Will you create a blog? If not, why? If yes, what is the name and tagline?

   _____

   _____

2. List one video and one podcast you could create to diversify your content. If you do not choose to do these, identify why.

   _____

   _____

3. Would joining a social network help your business grow? If so which one(s) and how?

   _____

   _____

4. Would it benefit your business to create an online community of your own? If so, which tool will you use and why?

   _____

   _____

5. Have you tried bookmarking or tagging sites? Can you see how you might integrate them into your plan?

   _____

   _____

6. Can you put customer reviews and or ratings on your website? How will you benefit from this?

   _____

   _____

Chapter 14

Step 6. Tactics—Tried and True

Do not wait for extraordinary circumstances to do good; try to use ordinary situations.
                    —John Paul Richter

▶ **Email Signatures**

▶ **Newsletters**

▶ **Article Marketing**

▶ **Online Press Releases**

▶ **White Papers**

▶ **Surveys and Polls**

▶ **Loyalty Programs**

▶ **Using a Success Ladder**

My definition of social media marketing includes using tried and true marketing tactics that include a social media twist whenever possible. The following are some traditional tactics you shouldn't forget about just because you're in a new online venue. They can be just as powerful using a social media twist. As we talk about each of the tactics in turn, we'll discuss what is important and how to get the most from each.

Email Signatures

Email signatures are about as old school as you can get, but that doesn't make them unimportant. Obviously, this tactic has been used since email was created, but that doesn't mean you should overlook it. Email signatures are little billboards for your products and services that appear naturally at the end of all your email communications.

Keys to a Good Email Signature

- Decide what your customers must know and only put that into your signature. This means excluding silly titles, unrelated degrees, and quotes to live by. Put in your name and your phone number. If you have a free item to promote, list it and make the link clickable. If you are promoting a blog and/or website, add that. That's it. The longer it is, the less likely anyone will read it.
- Try to keep it to six lines or less. You don't want the signature to be longer than the message itself.
- Skip the pictures unless you are a photographer.

Newsletters

Every book you read about online marketing urges you to create a newsletter. Generally, I agree. However, sending out a daily, weekly, or monthly newsletter takes a good deal of effort. Think through your newsletter strategy to determine if it's the right tactic for you. In some cases it may not be.

Before you decide, consider these questions:

- **What are your goals?** Are there other tactics that will help you reach these goals more effectively that you want to consider first?

- **How will you measure success?** If you don't know what the measures are, there's no point publishing just to say you have a newsletter.
- **How will you create and manage your mailing lists?** This is a key question. Don't start out doing this by hand if you have more than ten names—it will quickly usurp a lot of your time.
- **Can you develop meaningful content on an ongoing basis?** If you think a newsletter can be sustained by a list of products for sale, you are incorrect. That's a catalog, and you might want to consider that instead; a newsletter needs to have compelling content that describes and sells your products, not just a list of what's available.
- **Will you be able to ensure that everything is delivered correctly?** You need to be prepared to meet non-spam requirements.

QUICK Tip

Incorporating social media: With all the new technology available today, the term "newsletter" has morphed into a dozen different formats—it's no longer just sales copy sent to established customers. Using social media strategies like user-generated content can be a great way to make your newsletter stand out. For example, you can encourage users to send in their own articles and reviews, which can help build a strong base of readers. This works well when you have segmented and targeted your niches carefully.

Five Tips for Making Your Newsletter Great

1. Get an independent evaluation of your current newsletter strategy from a colleague or other marketer you trust. Make sure to discuss tangible success measurements. You need to know if what you are doing is actually worth continuing. Your communication with your customers needs to be personalized and targeted to sell, and newsletter content is no exception. Make sure your mailing list pays off.

2. Is a weekly or monthly format the right one? You may want something published regularly, or you may discover that a few targeted newsletters a year give you a greater return. Just like everything, you need to test and revise your newsletter and publication schedule to maximize the return.

3. Take advantage of new technology. There are new ways to personalize your content and develop a dialogue with your customers that won't be cost prohibitive. Consider using audio or video in your newsletter. Interviews and video how-to's can be very effective.

4. Make reading your newsletter pay off for your customer every time. Always offer discount links or other value-added information that separates your content from all the "value-free" content on the Web today. Think about what the reader will be interested in, not what your company wants to tell them. Think about what they want to BUY, not what you want to SELL.

5. Use your support area to launch new newsletters. Many e-commerce businesses miss an opportunity to communicate with their customers when they go to the support area. Customers want quick answers. They also like knowing that the company cares about what they want and need. A newsletter that focuses on FAQs and support would be a welcome change from all the "marketing" newsletters they receive. This idea is a simple one that only the most successful companies use. Don't overlook a way to stand out.

Alert!

Use those keywords: Make sure you use your keywords in your newsletter articles. Pay particular attention to the headlines you use—as with any other web content, you need to create attention-grabbing headlines using your keywords. One way to promote your newsletter on your site is to create a page with an archive of all the previous newsletters. Make sure the sign-up box is prominently displayed on that page. That way, you ensure that people who read samples will sign up. Also, put a sign-up box on every page of all your marketing channels.

Evaluating Your Newsletter's Success

If you plan to send email newsletters, you'll want to check out "Email Service Providers" (ESPs). These are companies that are in the business of sending online newsletters and making sure they get delivered. I use and recommend Constant Contact. It is a web-based email service provider that can help you create a professional-looking email campaign. It's easy to use and it does a good job of reporting your statistics. They have a free trial you can try to see if you like it at www.constantcontact.com. You might also try www.1shoppingcart.com, a vendor I also use, or www.exacttarget.com. The key to improving your newsletter campaigns is analyzing your statistics.

Constant Contact provides the following statistics to help you evaluate each issue of your newsletter:

- Number sent—How many people the email was sent to
- Bounces—How many people did not receive it because it was rejected as spam, their mailbox was full, or the address was faulty in some way.
- Spam Reports—How many people got your email and reported it as spam
- Opt-outs—How many people upon receiving your email decided to unsubscribe
- Opens—How many people actually opened the email you sent
- Clicks—How many people clicked on a link in your email or newsletter
- Forwards—How many people forwarded the email to a friend. For social media marketing campaigns, this is particularly telling.

If you don't have a way of tracking these measures, you really don't know how your content is being received.

QUICK Tip

Use each article to its fullest: To make sure search engines have updated content to spider on your site, take out each individual article in your newsletter and put it in your articles section. That way you will get added visibility in the search engines.

QUICK Tip

For information on how to establish and improve your newsletter, go to www.ezinequeen.com and sign up for Alexandria Brown's great newsletter. She's got lots of information to share.

Article Marketing

Article marketing is an important tactic for the small business owner. It has been overlooked because people feel that it takes too much time to write articles about their business and new products, and it's hard to see an immediate return.

However, article marketing is very important—it's a marketing tactic with real tangible benefits. It can get the right traffic to your site—buyers! It's a powerful lead generation tactic that attracts people interested in your topic. Get them to your website and you have a chance to develop a customer. Distribution of your articles by an article submission company is important to get them out and picked up by people who need content for newsletters, blogs, and article sites (more about that below).

There are three keys to creating articles that attract targeted traffic:

1. Careful selection of the right keyword phrases that target your audience—they need to be both in the headline and the body of the article.
2. Use of a distribution service to make sure the article gets wide distribution.
3. A "resource box" (the box at the end of the article that contains links to your site) that makes the best use of your links. Don't just send everyone to the home page.

Benefits of Article Marketing

One of the main benefits to article marketing is establishing backlinks. One of the ways search engines find you is by the volume of your backlinks, links that point back to your site from other places on the Web. The more backlinks you have, the higher you will rank on a results page.

QUICK Tip

Find your backlinks: To find out how many backlinks you already have on Google, go to Google.com and type in "info:Yourwebsitename". So, if your site were emarketer.com you would type in "info:emarketer.com". From here click on the link "Find web pages that link to emarketer.com." To see a more complete list, also scroll down to the link "web pages that contain the term." The reason the backlinks number is smaller than the pages that contain the term is that Google only reports the pages with a high ranking that link to you.

In the past, one of the ways that website owners would get backlinks is by looking at other sites and blogs with compatible audiences and sending them a request for a reciprocal link (each site puts a link on the other person's site). This way, you would generate more traffic to both sites. There is nothing wrong with this method. If you know of sites that are complimentary, by all means send an email request to trade links.

Producing Quality Articles

It requires a bit of effort to continually generate quality articles, but it's worth it. There are several ways to generate articles:

- Take all the press releases, white papers, and other content you have and turn them into articles.
- Repurpose your newsletter content into articles.
- Repurpose your blog posts into articles. (Make sure to vary the content so it's not exactly the same.)
- Hire someone to write articles for you on a regular basis.

In order to help make it easy for my clients to use article marketing, I have developed a five step process that makes it easy for you to write plenty of articles—you need to approach it in a mechanical way. Here is a step-by-step process that lets you figure out what kind of article you need to write to suit your purpose, and helps you write it. I also created a Mind Map that shows you the big picture of these steps so you can follow them visually (see Figure 14.1).

Figure 14.1

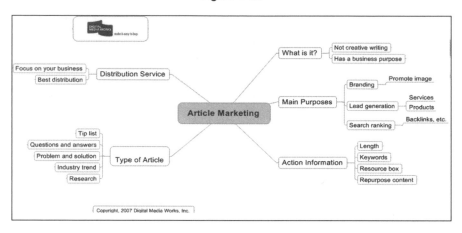

1. Start by focusing on how to think about article marketing:

First, you need to understand that article writing is marketing, not creative writing—it has to serve a business purpose. You don't have to worry about all the things you fear about writing; the quality of information is key, not the great prose. Focusing on the business purpose should help you determine what to write.

2. Decide which of the three main business purposes you are focusing on:

Branding—Promote the company's image and expertise. We all know that a brand is how companies distinguish their product from others in the market. Your brand is what the company stands for, your values translated into action. To write an article for this purpose, concentrate on how your new product or service upholds your high standards.

Lead generation—Demonstrate that you have the knowledge to solve a particular problem. If you're promoting a service, spell out the problem it addresses and how you approach its solution, as well as how you've worked with others on the same problem. If you're selling a product, provide information about how a product like yours is used. (For example if you are selling speakers, you can talk about the five top ways to make speakers sound good.)

Improved search engine ranking and increased site traffic—If this is the goal of your article marketing, the key here is not the article you write but the amount of articles you write. Five to ten articles aren't enough—this takes time, don't get discouraged. Just keep writing.

3. Determine keywords, resource box, and article length.
Ask yourself:

Which keywords am I promoting?

How long will the article be? (About three hundred to six hundred words for most newsletters. If it's too long, break it into two parts.)

What do I need to put in my resource box?

What is the call to action that relates to this article—what do I want the customer to do after reading it?

4. What type of article will best serve my purpose?
Now that you know what and why you're writing, what kind of format serves the information best? Should you put it into tip lists, question and answer format, or is it more like a straight research article? Try to match the format to the content; it will help the information be more accessible to the reader.

5. Submit your article to a distribution service.
You will want to use an article submission company to distribute your articles. I like www.ezinearticles.com. They do a great job of distributing your articles to the widest possible audience, and it's free to join. You might also try www.articlemarketer.com. They offer a variety of plans to suit your needs. It's easier to submit your articles to a service and let them do the distribution, rather than do each submission by hand. It's better to spend the time you save writing more articles.

Online Press Releases
In the current Web environment, two-way communication is the key to being found and respected. Press releases have taken on a more important role with Web 2.0 because they function as a way to increase your standing in the search engines as well as speak to the media and potential customers.

One can no longer think about press releases as a closed path to the media. They are not just for the press—they can be seen and read by anyone interested in your message.

Like any other form of online communication, keywords figure prominently in a press release. Building a database of media contacts can be as simple as noting who writes about your topic or product on a regular basis. Put these names and addresses in a database along with influential bloggers and other media industry stars. There are also several online distribution companies you can use. www.BusinessWire.com and www.PRNewswire .com are two. Another unique company you may wish to check out is ExpertClick.com.

ExpertClick: ExpertClick is a subscription service that gives you an online contact platform—basically, you post your info and press releases, and they make sure it gets to all the places it needs to be. When you join, they give you a "Press Room Page" on which you can put your photo, important website links, and multimedia. Included in the subscription is the ability to send fifty-two press releases at no extra cost. Their annual membership is cost-effective and the press releases go to News Release Wire and other outlets. You are included in their printed Yearbook of Experts that is also searchable online. The media can receive these free of charge. If this service sounds interesting, go to www.expertclick.com/ brochure and check it out.

Effective Press Releases

There is no magic formula to make people pay attention to your release, but there are things you should do. Here are five ways to maximize the success of each press release you send:

1. Determine the target audience.

Be clear about the segment of your list that the release is targeted to, and send it only to them.

2. Identify your specific keywords for this release.

Chose the top three or four keywords that must be in the release you are sending—pay particular attention to your headline and subhead. Make sure that your keywords flow smoothly and don't seem out of place; a headline that awkwardly brandishes a string of keywords will repel people, particularly journalists.

3. Send and/or build a central information repository for the topic it covers.

Include content links that will take your reader to more information on the subject of your press release. When appropriate, I have my clients create landing pages just for a special release about a new product or service. That includes podcasts, video, and other pertinent content.

4. Distribute widely.

Distribute your release using a professional service like PRWeb.

5. Analyze your traffic.

Analyze the responses to determine the popularity of your topic. Also, find out who followed up on the release and how they got it.

White Papers

White papers are an easy concept to understand and a difficult one to execute well. What is a white paper? Merriam-Webster defines a white paper as simply "a detailed or authoritative report." White papers are key for companies who have a long sales cycle or complex products. They provide an argument and success statistics.

There are two issues that are important when it comes to white papers: (1) making sure they are easily found; and (2) making them readable once they are found. You need a balance between a document that is easy to read and something with enough information and substance to make your case.

If your industry competes using white papers, you have no choice but to make them compelling. If you feel you can't create something suitable, look into hiring someone to help.

CASE STUDY: Three questions for Michael A. Stelzner, author of the best-selling book *Writing White Papers: How to Capture Readers and Keep Them Engaged*

1. **Michael, with the advent of exciting social media options, why do you think online marketers should still use white papers?**

   Social media will never replace the need for white papers. The fact that websites like Digg.com point people to great content will only increase the value of white papers. You see, people use white papers to help them make decisions. White papers are the oldest tools in the marketing arsenal. They are highly educational and allow businesses to make the case about why their approach is superior.

2. **How can readers enhance their white papers with social media tactics?**

   The combination of white papers and social media is a very new phenomenon. Podcasting is one way that marketers can drive traffic to their white papers. The idea is to simply create a ten-minute podcast, interviewing the experts and creating interest in the white paper. White papers are also very useful on blogs. I have seen many marketers include a thumbnail image of their white paper on their blog. The thumbnail points to a simple registration page to get the white paper via email—which means you'll also get the interested party's email address for future contact.

3. **What is the one tip you would give anyone planning to use white papers as a marketing tactic?**

   My number one tip for white papers is to hide them behind a registration form—not just any landing page, one rich with content. Take the first two pages of the paper and format the text like an article. Once a reader is hooked and scrolls down, registration is required to access the rest of the paper. When a lead arrives, it is prequalified because the content was valuable AND read prior to the registration. The result is better leads.

Additional Resources: For more about white papers, sign up for Michael's newsletter and receive a free sample chapter of his book at www.writing-whitepapers.com/newsletter.html. Also, check out Michael's blog at www.writingwhitepapers.com/blog/.

Surveys and Polls

Polling subscribers to your newsletter, blog, or other marketing channels for suggestions and ideas for improvement is a good idea. Frequently, my clients say they prefer not to do polls because they are afraid that not many people will respond. Don't let that discourage you. You're not looking for quantity, you're looking for quality.

People who answer surveys are motivated to give you their ideas and feedback—they feel passionate enough about some aspect of your business to take the time to answer you. You can always learn something from it. Develop a thicker skin and try it. Ask them real questions whose answers have meaning to you. When people see a request for a survey they need to feel that the answers will be read and acted upon by the surveyor. Don't create a list of bland, uninteresting questions that no one, including you, cares about.

A free tool you can use to create a survey for under one hundred respondents per poll is found at www.Surveymonkey.com. If you use an email service like Constant Contact, they have a polling feature. If you want to create a free poll from your blog, check out www.Vizu.com and www.Blogpolls.com.

Loyalty Programs

Loyalty programs are not new. They are discount programs that give customers an increasing benefit for shopping at a retail store. High-end retailers have relied on these for years; for instance, Neiman Marcus has had their InCircle program in place for more than twenty-five years. But, with the customer's newfound control, loyalty programs are taking a new shape.

Alert!

Spice up the program: Shoppers are looking for a unique experience beyond the usual discounts and points. In 2007, Nordstrom rolled out a new loyalty program called Fashion Rewards. It lets customers design shopping trips and provides other perks, such as access to a private fashion emergency "hot line." The customer is exerting greater control over the types of rewards and benefits she'll receive. This is something you need to give thought to. Is there some way you can provide your customer with an experience rather than just a discount?

Using a Success Ladder

Finally, I want to briefly discuss a tactic that will help you increase your business and do some good as well. How about using your online business as a success ladder to create opportunities for others? If you succeed in this, you also might get business from people who want to work with you because of your generosity.

What do I mean by a success ladder? Visualize a ladder: you are on the rungs, giving others a boost to get above you. This doesn't mean you are staying at the bottom. It means that as you rise, you are helping others to reach greater heights. This makes it possible for everyone to rise higher. This is something that can bring you great satisfaction.

Online, you can reach people and do things you never dreamed possible as a small business owner. The Web makes it easy for people to collaborate, and a success ladder is about mutually aiding and promoting others. Think about networking activities that can give someone a boost—they can also give you a boost, in both reciprocal promotion and reputation. You're not expecting to measure this in dollars, so the pressure is off.

CASE STUDY: Climbing the success ladder

Timberland shoe apparel company CEO Jeffrey B. Swartz has seen first-hand how developing a success ladder can be rewarding for his company and the community at large. Timberland began helping City Year, a youth service corps in Boston, by providing boots for corps members. An article in 2005 by the Chronicle of Philanthropy reported on a speech given by Mr. Swartz, in which he discussed the evolution of his relationship with City Year. He believes that putting in the time to develop a vision and a strategic relationship with City Year made all the difference. As Timberland's community involvement has grown, so have its profits, which Mr. Swartz said is not a coincidence: "It is not a factor of my brilliant strategic leadership…It directly correlates to the fact that people at Timberland are mission-centered, passionate people." In 2007 the relationship is going strong with a new City Year in New Hampshire, where Timberland is headquartered.

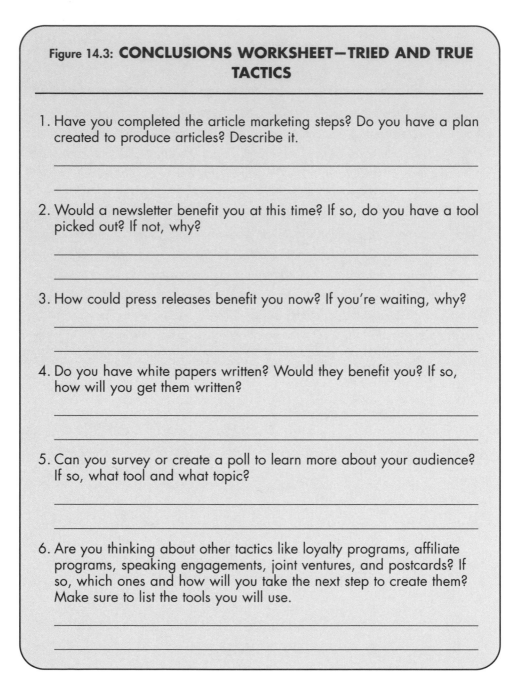

Figure 14.3: CONCLUSIONS WORKSHEET—TRIED AND TRUE TACTICS

1. Have you completed the article marketing steps? Do you have a plan created to produce articles? Describe it.

2. Would a newsletter benefit you at this time? If so, do you have a tool picked out? If not, why?

3. How could press releases benefit you now? If you're waiting, why?

4. Do you have white papers written? Would they benefit you? If so, how will you get them written?

5. Can you survey or create a poll to learn more about your audience? If so, what tool and what topic?

6. Are you thinking about other tactics like loyalty programs, affiliate programs, speaking engagements, joint ventures, and postcards? If so, which ones and how will you take the next step to create them? Make sure to list the tools you will use.

Step 7. Results

In the fields of observation, chance favors only the prepared mind.

—Louis Pasteur

▶ **What Gets Measured Gets Done**

▶ **Using Web Analytics**

▶ **What to Track**

Web analytics is a subject most business people try to avoid. Measuring how visitors use your website, how many blog readers you have, who buys, and under what conditions seems both complex and boring. I have spoken to many CEOs and Directors of all size companies who base their web analysis on their "gut feelings." They decide how they feel and find bits of revenue data to support those feelings. Scientific, it's not—and just so you know, I am not basing this on my "intuition." *Revenue Magazine*, May/June 2007, reports on findings from Jupiter Research that only 5 percent of companies planning online campaigns use analytics, and 69 percent planning campaigns use "intuition" in place of analytics.

You're in the majority if you shy away from using analytics. However, not doing so is a big mistake, and if you use it, you're ahead of most of the other companies out there.

What Gets Measured Gets Done

As business guru Tom Peters has said, "What gets measured gets done." If you don't know how visitors are interacting with your website, you can't do anything to effect change. You are reacting instead of planning. The number of visitors to your website divided by the number of people who buy is just the tip of the iceberg of information you can find.

If you learn to love this topic, you will have a leg up on the competition. You know your business well, and intuitively understand what needs to be done to make it successful—but you need data to help you decide what changes to your online marketing efforts will have the most impact.

Several of the social media marketing tactics make it hard to track rate of return because their effects are cumulative. By using analytics data, you can at least see the strengths and weaknesses of each tactic and determine what needs beefing up. There is nothing wrong with using your intuition, but having the data to back it up can turn your good ideas into great ones.

Using Web Analytics

Web analytics refers to the measurement of the actions your customers take as they move around your website. Most people who have a website or blog hosted online have a statistics package included. It is generally hard to read and loaded with items you can't identify, much less use to your advantage. Most people don't have the time or the inclination to pore over these statistics. If anyone in the company asks for them, they get a big dump of a file. Good luck making that work for you! I'm not saying you can't use it—I'm saying you probably don't use it.

For this reason, web analytics companies sprang up to meet the unfulfilled need for usable analytics. These tools are visual and easier to read, but the price is sometimes out of reach of the small business owner who is struggling to stay even.

Google Analytics—Getting Started

In 2005, Google purchased a small company that tracked web data called Urchin. Everyone waited to see what would happen. The tool was good and with Google's technologies and resources it had the potential to be very good.

In 2006 it was rebranded Google Analytics—and made available free. The demand was huge. The tool is still free today and considered the de facto standard for small businesses and entrepreneurs. It is available at www.google.com/analytics.

There are many good website analytic tools available to you now. Obviously, I recommend that you try Google Analytics first. You can always spend money on a higher-end package later, if you deem it necessary. If you don't have an account with Google, you'll need to set one up. If you already signed up for a Gmail account or use AdWords, you're all set.

The first key to using Google Analytics successfully (or any analytics program) is to make sure it's set up correctly. Don't skip over this. If you don't set it up correctly you'll be wasting valuable time and data. If you are not up to speed on HTML and don't have an in-house person, hire a trusted outside developer or Google-certified analyst to do it. It should be quick and inexpensive.

QUICK Tip

Use the tracking code everywhere: Make sure that you or your developer remembers to put the tracking code on every page you want to track—not just the home page. When you add new pages, make sure to add the tracking code. The tracking code is the part of the analytics program that actually records usage.

Once it's set up, you can start looking at your data. At the very beginning you won't have enough data to draw definitive conclusions, but you will be able to see patterns and identify data points for further investigation. Once you have about a month's worth of data, you can begin to see what works about your online marketing, what doesn't, and start brainstorming solutions as you collect more data.

What to Track

Here are five statistics I think it's critical to know, regardless of what type of business you have:

- Key Performance Indicators (KPI)—these measurements are specific to the health of your business and vary from company to company. Make a list of your three most important goals and create measurements to track them. If your number one goal is email newsletter signups, for instance, make sure you know how many you get a day, and from what page on your site.
- Average pages viewed per visit
- Average time spent on the site
- Bounce rate (the percentage of visitors who look at one page and leave the site)
- Percentage of repeat vs. new visitors

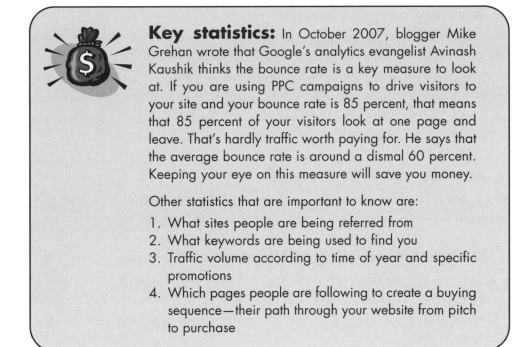

Key statistics: In October 2007, blogger Mike Grehan wrote that Google's analytics evangelist Avinash Kaushik thinks the bounce rate is a key measure to look at. If you are using PPC campaigns to drive visitors to your site and your bounce rate is 85 percent, that means that 85 percent of your visitors look at one page and leave. That's hardly traffic worth paying for. He says that the average bounce rate is around a dismal 60 percent. Keeping your eye on this measure will save you money.

Other statistics that are important to know are:

1. What sites people are being referred from
2. What keywords are being used to find you
3. Traffic volume according to time of year and specific promotions
4. Which pages people are following to create a buying sequence—their path through your website from pitch to purchase

Using the Statistics

Don't forget that the purpose of analyzing web traffic is to see how you can improve it. If you just look at the stats and take no action, then you are missing an opportunity to grow your business.

Once you are up and running for a while there are some common problems to watch out for. They include:

• Traffic not converting

A lot of traffic means nothing if you aren't getting them to buy. Don't be excited just because your traffic numbers are high. You need to see revenue or your desired response attached in good ratio to the number of visitors.

• High bounce rate

This relates to traffic volume. If you have lots of visits but they leave after looking at one page, you don't have the most targeted audience for you.

• Very few pages visited

Are all your visitors going to the same few pages and then leaving? You have enough content to get them to follow a path; you just don't have the converting content yet. Look at the analytics to see where they drop off. Add more content to the pages that follow until you have a winning combination and a good percentage of your visitors are following the path all the way through to a purchase.

• Balance of traffic skewed

If you see that all of your traffic is coming from search engines and very little from referrals or visa versa, you need to beef up your efforts in that area.

• Broken links driving traffic away

This seems like an obvious one, but very few people check their links to make sure they all work. There are lots of dead link checkers you can use. Here's one that you can try: http://www.dead-links.com/check_ links.php.

CASE STUDY: **Three questions for Michael Harrison, a web analytics and optimization specialist at ROIrevolution.com, a Google Analytics Authorized and AdWords Qualified online marketing consultancy**

---

1. Michael, how has the development of so many new social media tools impacted web analytics?

As content on the Internet becomes easier for people to share, it's useful for businesses to understand how visitors arrive at their websites. I can share a link on Digg or Facebook and it has the potential to generate huge amounts of traffic for that site.

Your average web user may encounter multiple links to a single site in just a day, as they check email, read RSS feeds, and check up on their MySpace pages. Sorting the wheat from the chaff becomes important.

2. How should small businesses approach analytics to get the most from using them?

Come up with a list of actionable questions about your site. These are questions that should be answered by any data that is collected. "Do I need to reduce spending on AdWords?" "Are SEO costs justifiable?" "Which blog articles are people sharing?" When the data collects, you'll know what changes to make.

3. What is the one tip you would give anyone planning to use Google Analytics?

Don't put the Google Analytics Tracking Code on your site right away. Google Analytics is easy to set up and use, but if you configure it incorrectly, the data it collects will be faulty. Bad data is worse than no data at all. Get someone who knows what they're doing to inspect your configuration. Then tag your pages.

Additional Resources: Michael is also a founding contributor to the ROI Revolution Unofficial Google Analytics Blog (www.roirevolution.com/blog) and an instructor in ROI Revolution's weekly Google Analytics Training Series (www.roirevolution.com/google-analytics/training).

Figure 15.1: CONCLUSIONS WORKSHEET—RESULTS

1. Have you used web analytics in the past? If not, why not?

   _____

   _____

2. List the benefits you'll get from using web analytics now.

   _____

   _____

3. Which tool will you use for your web analytics? Is it set up? If not, how will you get it set up?

   _____

   _____

4. What measures will you track? List at least five.

   _____

   _____

5. Which other marketing channels will you track, like your blog, newsletter, etc.?

   _____

   _____

Section IV
Completed Plan and Beyond

Chapter 16

Putting It All Together

It is better to know some of the questions than all of the answers

—*James Thurber*

▶ **Analyze Your Time vs. Revenue**

▶ **Questions to Ask**

▶ **Putting the Plan Together**

Before you start putting your marketing plan together, it's valuable to look at how you are spending your work time. Taking the time to look at priorities will, of course, make you more productive. But, this analysis goes deeper. You need to take a "big picture" look at how you spend your time at work and then adjust it to get the greatest revenue return.

Analyze Your Time vs. Revenue

Before you determine how to revise how you spend your time, you need to figure out where you're currently spending your time. Once you know that, you need to focus on how to make the time you spend working generate more revenue. I created a worksheet called Time vs. Revenue Assessment to do this. Complete the Time vs. Revenue Worksheet and then move to the questions in the next section.

Figure 16.1: TIME VS. REVENUE ASSESSMENT

1. Start by listing the five activities that bring in the most revenue on a monthly basis. These could be products, ad revenue, royalties, consulting fees, etc.

   1. _____
   2. _____
   3. _____
   4. _____
   5. _____

2. List the five activities that bring you the most traffic. These could be blogs, newsletters, social networking, etc.

   1. _____
   2. _____
   3. _____
   4. _____
   5. _____

3. Of those that generate traffic, which ones can you definitively say translate into direct revenue?

1. _____

2. _____

3. _____

4. _____

5. _____

4. Of those that don't generate direct revenue, which ones have the most potential to generate direct revenue?

1. _____

2. _____

3. _____

4. _____

5. _____

5. Which activities do I spend time on that have no potential to generate revenue or support revenue generation?

1. _____

2. _____

3. _____

4. _____

5. _____

Questions to Ask

Business guru Brian Tracy asks four questions of his clients to help them determine the best use of their time. I've added one to his list. Don't be surprised if these questions seem simple—they are deceptively simple. These are things that you probably aren't thinking about as much as you should. Use the worksheet you just filled out to help you pinpoint the exact activities you should focus on.

1. What am I doing that I should be doing more of?

The things that generate the most revenue need to be analyzed and expanded upon. If you have one or two products that generate most of the revenue, figure out how to bundle additional items to create new and compelling offers, like regular, deluxe, and professional packages. You get the idea. Also, analyze what your customers are responding to in those offers and try to create new products with the same hook.

2. What am I doing that I should be doing less of?

All the things you do that are not listed as answers to questions one to four of the Time vs. Revenue Assessment worksheet should be scrutinized. They are not bringing you revenue, traffic, nor do they have the potential to. They seem like good items to do less of.

3. What am I not doing that I should start doing?

Look at the list you created in question four of the worksheet. Those items that you listed are those that have the most potential. You should start to ramp up the work that you do on them to see if they really can generate direct revenue.

4. What am I doing that I should stop doing?

Look at your answers to question five of the worksheet and take a hard look at where you're wasting your time. When you realize that you are doing certain activities that are generating no actual return, you need to put a stop to them. They have no value to your company.

5. What am I doing to self-promote my business and learn about the work of my colleagues?

It's important to evaluate whether you spend some part of your day self-promoting or "talking up" your business. Throughout the day you speak to vendors, partners, potential customers, etc., just to touch base, see if they have any concerns or suggestions, and fill them in on any new developments.

Some portion of that conversation, however brief, should be devoted to asking how their business is doing and telling them how yours is doing. I don't mean a big sales pitch or false bravado. Everyone sees through that and it can appear desperate. It also doesn't mean asking a perfunctory, "how are you" and not listening to the answer. It means being genuinely interested in what they are doing and letting them know what new or exciting things you are up to. That's worth your time and will pay dividends. You are apt to learn of a new project you might be able to cross-promote with, or you may spur a colleague's interest in something new you are doing and get their participation. Self-promotion, when done well, is a two-way street that helps build communication and open doors to new opportunities.

Putting the Plan Together

You've worked on analyzing your activities and collecting information about strategies and tactics. You know what works in your online marketing plan and what doesn't, and you've brainstormed possible improvements. You're exploring new venues for social media marketing. Now you're ready to put your 7 Step Action Plan together.

If you filled out the conclusion sheets as you went along, you should have all the information you need to complete your plan.

First you need to fill out Figure 16.2, the New Mindset Worksheet. Compare it with Worksheet 7.1: Present State and Worksheet 7.2: Present Mindset to see how your mindset has changed.

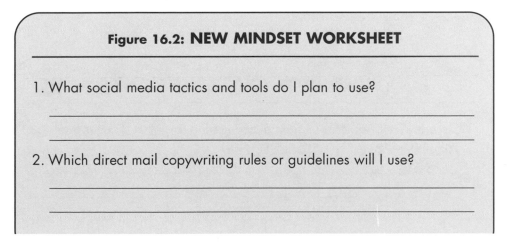

Figure 16.2: NEW MINDSET WORKSHEET

1. What social media tactics and tools do I plan to use?

2. Which direct mail copywriting rules or guidelines will I use?

3. What User-Generated Content can I use to get feedback from customers?

_____

_____

4. Are there new ways I plan to collaborate online with employees or partners?

_____

_____

5. Who is on my targeted list of influencers?

_____

_____

6. Do I have any new ideas about how to innovate?

_____

_____

Now you're ready to fill out worksheet "Your 7 Step Plan Complete" using all the information you collected in your conclusion sheets. The purpose of this worksheet is to have one place where you can look at your entire plan as a cohesive whole.

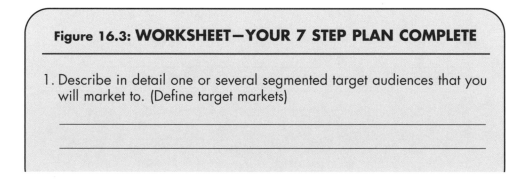

Figure 16.3: **WORKSHEET—YOUR 7 STEP PLAN COMPLETE**

1. Describe in detail one or several segmented target audiences that you will market to. (Define target markets)

_____

_____

2. How are you positioning your company? Do you have a tagline for it? How will customers think about your brand? (Define your position)

_____

_____

3. What is your company's story? (Develop your story)

_____

_____

4. List the types of content formats you will provide online (e.g., podcast, video).

   (Website Content)

_____

_____

5. What is the search strategy that makes it easy for your customer to find you? (What tools, what keywords, etc.) (Keywords and Search Engines)

_____

_____

6. What tactics have you chosen (both social media and tried and true) to generate more revenue? (Tactics)

_____

_____

7. What measurements will you use to analyze actions taken by customers? (Results)

_____

_____

QUICK Tip

Make a Mind Map of your action plan: I would also recommend making a Mind Map of your plan and posting it near your workspace so you don't lose sight of what you're trying to accomplish. Review the map and worksheet in three months and see how far you've come and how you can modify it to grow even more.

Chapter  17

Let the Message Work for You

There is only one thing in the world worse than being talked about and that is not being talked about.

—Oscar Wilde

▶ **New Ways to Reach an Audience**

▶ **What is the Role of Influencers?**

▶ **Creating a WOM Campaign**

▶ **Mobile Marketing**

We know that the ability to share stories using video, audio, bookmarking, and a host of other techniques helps people stay connected on the Web. You have a story that you want your customers to tell. These stories include why someone likes using your product, how they found it, and why they want to recommend it to others. How can you encourage the spread of your stories?

New Ways to Reach an Audience

The very fact that people can easily communicate across the globe makes your message and the way people spread it a more important factor than ever before. A survey done in 2005 by CNW Marketing Research found that more than 40 percent of all the TV ads for major items like cars, credit cards, fast food, and pet products are ignored by TV viewers. That's almost half of all the advertising!

So, advertisers have to find new ways to get your attention. That's why they've turned to such tools as blogs, online communities, and social networks. They want to speak directly to the consumer in a channel that is not encumbered by "ad speak." People who use Facebook, MySpace, and other social networks are hyper-vigilant about spotting blatant advertisements and stopping them in their tracks. You certainly don't want to use those tactics. They build a wall between you and your audience and they don't work.

As you look at the different ways to get your message out organically, without using ads or other marketing tactics, you see that most of it is out of your control. That's what makes social media marketing different from traditional marketing. What is in your control is the quality of your product. If you make your product or service worth talking about, you make it easy to spread the word. If you also provide ways for people to get that message out, you've done it all.

Here are some ideas about how to get your message out:

- Develop a group of affiliates who carry your message.
- Make speeches to associations and at trade shows.
- Create a vignette about your product for your blogs, newsletters, message boards, and discussion groups.
- Solicit opinions in your own and other online communities where you can get product ideas and feedback.

- Find high profile influencers from other blogs, media, and association sites.
- Send out postcards or other snail mail.
- Do interviews on Internet radio shows and podcasts.

When you are considering how you will encourage customers to talk about you, you need to understand the difference between WOM, Viral Marketing, and Buzz.

Word-of-Mouth Marketing

Word-of-mouth marketing (WOM) refers to the spread of your brand message from person to person—it is the act of talking about and referring a product or service to others. This method is slow, but consistent—when people get a product referral from someone they know, they are likely to follow it. A typical word-of-mouth example includes the recommendation from a friend about a new software program or insurance deal.

Alert!

The importance of WOM: A 2004 RoperASW report says that 90 percent of Americans consider WOM their best source of ideas and information. They consider WOM twice as important as advertising and place 1.5 times more value on it than they did twenty-five years ago.

In a Nielsen survey done worldwide in April 2007, the top four types of advertising trusted by Internet users were:

- Recommendations from consumers
- Newspapers
- Consumer opinions posted online
- Brand websites

Note that the brand sites come in behind both consumer opinions and recommendations—people no longer trust only what a company tells them about their product, but look for what independent consumers have to say about it.

CASE STUDY: Generating word-of-mouth advertising

Some marketing companies have sprung up that are helping manufacturers tap into the opinions of influential people, with the goal of creating more targeted products to facilitate WOM advertising. eMarketer estimated that in 2007 there were 26.8 million Internet users in the U.S. considered to be "WOM influencers." Their impact can be significant.

Screenlife Games, the maker of Scene It? (a DVD movie game), hired BuzzLogic, a company that assists corporations in harnessing their social media strategy, to increase the sales of their product American Idol—All Star Challenge. BuzzLogic analyzed blogs, videos, and other online material that existed about the show and selected an online panel of influencers. From this group they were able to find out what was most important to the potential buyers of the product and created a product specifically targeted to their needs. This group of influencers then went on to recommend the product they helped to develop. This differs from using a focus group that gives their opinions but has no major outlet to bring the message to others.

Viral Marketing

Like WOM, viral marketing is an idea that spreads from one person to another. It differs from WOM in that it spreads faster and has a higher profile. For example, when Harry Potter books were first published in the U.S., there was very little fanfare. The series gained momentum as kids told their friends about it, and that momentum built quickly. Contrast the release of the first book with the release of the final installment of the series—in the first twenty-four hours, 8.3 million copies of the last book in the series were sold in the U.S. alone.

> **Be careful when going viral:** Information spread virally can be good or bad. When something you are selling or promoting goes viral, that's great. When a customer uploads a YouTube video of your on-site staffer sleeping instead of working, you will have a different view of viral messages.

Competitrack, a company that tracks viral marketing campaigns, defines viral marketing as "online messages that are aimed primarily at attracting and engaging an audience, and secondarily at supporting a brand or product." It's a more targeted approach than word-of-mouth.

Competitrack reports that the top ten viral brands are:

Nike
Anheuser-Busch
Microsoft
Volkswagen
Axe
Apple
Coca-Cola
Adidas
PepsiCo
McDonald's

Buzz

Buzz is viral marketing on steroids—buzz spreads like fire because it generally includes a celebrity or high profile story. What you see on tabloid TV shows and read in celebrity newspapers is buzz. It comes and goes quickly—there is momentary excitement and then everyone is off to the next story, but that momentary excitement might be very profitable.

Since you may not have celebrity endorsements for your product or be the buzz of the day, you can work to tie your message to current events that contain those elements. For example, you can create a blog post that ties a big news story in with your product to get some attention.

CASE STUDY: Marketing your message

Money Management International is a non-profit service company that offers financial guidance for budgeting, money management, and credit issues. In November 2006, they wanted to find a way to show consumers how to spend responsibly during the holiday season. They came up with the idea of creating a minisite called Regiftable.com where people could share their regifting stories, and learn about how to give people gifts other than money. According to the Word of Mouth Marketing Association, Regiftable.com generated almost six hundred media exposures and seven hundred regifting stories which translated into over 230 million media impressions. Clearly, by taking a more creative approach to holiday spending, they were able to reach many more people with their message.

What is the Role of Influencers?

In 2007, the role of influencers became a hot topic. Previously, there was a rush to accept the notion that "influentials" actually created a market. But now there is evidence to the contrary. Some marketers argue that influentials are not creating trends; they are driving ideas that are nascent. That is, they are tapping into something that is erupting—not creating its success, but recommending it.

It is important for you take note of this distinction, when you consider your WOM campaigns. It should change your approach. Ed Keller and Jon Berry, authors of *The Influentials*, have said that influencers are "not the early adopters, they are the early majority." Previously, people would court influencers as though they owned a new idea. Now, influencers are seen as those who are vocal about something that is in the process of becoming mainstream.

Alert!

Don't replace planning with influencers: You need influencers to champion your products, but you also need to be aware of the conditions influencing your business and how you can make that work for you. You want to start the plan for your campaign by looking at what trends and ideas are taking root, rather than just who is speaking the loudest.

Janet Edan-Harris, CEO of Umbria, a company that monitors online buzz, agrees. Quoted in *Information Week* she said, "It's much more important to identify those themes that are gaining momentum than try to find opinion leaders...You want to ride the wave rather than trying to start one on your own."

Types of Influencers

Now that you know the different levels of grassroots marketing, it's important to look at influencer types so you can target them effectively. Malcolm Gladwell popularized three types of influencers in his book *The Tipping Point*. They are:

- **Connectors:** people who know a great many people and delight in bringing them together. Their value is not only who they know, it's also the different types of people they know.
- **Mavens:** those dedicated to accumulating knowledge and sharing it with others. Their goal is to learn as much as possible and educate as many people as they can. If you are lucky enough to know one, you nurture that relationship because Mavens do not try to persuade you to agree with them. Their goal is to provide knowledge in the hope that it will enrich your life, not convince you to agree with their opinion.
- **Salesmen:** these are the persuaders. They always know the best restaurants, the coolest shoes, and the best vacation spots to visit. Their goal is to persuade you to believe what they believe. Their goal is to sell you their ideas, both literally and figuratively.

Choosing Your Influencers

In addition to segmenting the different types of influencers, you should also organize them with regard to their spheres of influence—those who influence their local community, those who impact a larger audience online, and those who are members of the media. All three are important to you. Some people to consider:

1. Local community leaders

There are the community leaders who have influence in their small groups. According to a RoperASW study of influentials in 2003, these leaders are likely to be active in professional organizations. They are willing to complain when they don't get satisfaction from a product, and they are eager to learn new things.

2. Online opinion leaders

Bloggers, online community members, people who frequent discussion boards—these people have an influence over your particular audience if they're writing in forums that your customers frequent. Positive reviews from online opinion leaders can be very important.

3. Media

The media's job is to report on the latest trends, ideas and information. The media has influence over a vast majority of people in many different venues.

CASE STUDY: Classic car collectors

If you think that the price of your product will limit your ability to encourage WOM, consider high-end "collector's clubs." These clubs cater to people with the passion for an object and the ability to pay for the finest examples of it.

In August 2007, the Wall Street Journal reported on classic car collectors as a prime example. One member is quoted as saying, "Car collecting is built on networking. People know each other." These car prices can range into the millions and WOM is one of the primary ways they get found and sold.

How to find influencers

You need to survey the field and find the people you believe are potential influencers. You can go to online forums, Technorati.com, and online communities to start a list. From this list you need to do further research and winnow it down. You should take the time to determine if these are the people who matter to your products and services. If you pick those with little actual influence in your area, your effort will be ineffective.

And, of course, don't forget about offline influencers. You'll find them at trade shows, speaking engagements, in associations, shopping malls, public forums, etc. According to a December 4, 2006, article in *Advertising Age* by Ed Keller and Jon Berry, "90 percent of WOM conversations occur face to face or by phone vs. only 7 percent online." This means that you should be budgeting for all types of WOM when you launch a new product. If appropriate, create an event or promotion where customers can meet and share information.

QUICK Tip

Working with influencers:

When you work with influencers remember to:

1. Let them steer you in the right direction.

2. Listen to what they say, positive and negative.

3. Let them in on previews of new products.

4. Understand their values and beliefs.

Where do influencers get their information?

This is a key question, and you want the answer. The best way to find out is to ask. When you are talking to an influencer, make sure to ask her where she finds information. Then you can make sure to look at those sources and perhaps advertise there. In 2007, Yahoo and Mediavest did a study of consumers called "Passionista: The New Empowered Consumers." They define Passionistas as Internet users who spend a lot of time looking at information and brands that are associated with their passion. How do these Passionistas spend their time online when specifically pursuing their passion?

According to the study:

- 38 percent used a search engine to look for content.
- 23 percent sent an email or instant message to someone.
- 11 percent posted messages on user-created sites/boards.
- 11 percent submitted comments on stories or posts online.

This suggests that organic search, emails, user-created sites, and blogs are all good places to find and speak to your influencer.

Creating a WOM Campaign

To develop an effective WOM campaign you need to determine:

1. the state of the market and what trends fit
2. the current message being spread about you
3. how you want to revise the message or build on it
4. your niches and how best to reach them
5. which tactics you'll use
6. how you'll test the message

One way to get a WOM campaign going is to "seed" the market with samples of your product. Seeding can speed up the transmission of information by directly encouraging people to use your product or service at no charge. You can give away a free sample, an e-book that shows your expertise, a trial download of your software product, or a free half-hour consultation. The key is to plant a seed.

How to encourage good WOM

Guy Kawasaki, well known Mac Evangelist and author of *The Art of the Start*, calls people who love and evangelize your products "thunderlizards." Put your thunderlizards to work! Give them a personal view of your company and products. How do you know if the person you are considering is an influential? They are the ones who want to be up on the fads, first to know of new products, and excited to spread the word.

Some activities you can engage influencers in to help them spread the word:

- Interview them and post a podcast of the interview on your site.
- Let them be a guest article writer for your newsletter.
- Have them create an audio testimonial.
- Give them a discount coupon to provide to the audiences they influence.
- Ask them to be a teleseminar guest for your online community.
- Offer to write an article for their newsletter or blog.
- Get referrals to other bloggers the influencer thinks would be interested in your products.
- See if the influencer has any other ideas about joint ventures.

CASE STUDY: Corporations jump on board

Large corporations like Proctor & Gamble and Del Monte have taken an aggressive approach to building WOM. Their approach is to actively create an online community rather than wait for one to form. They make it easy for customers to talk to one another and spread the word.

Proctor & Gamble created a website called VocalPoint.com at which their members "get access to fun, thought-provoking experiences and explore products and services." A 2006 BusinessWeek article described this group as "a stealth army of six hundred thousand moms who chat up its (P&G) products." Some media argue that consumers organized and led by the company itself can not spread unbiased information, but either way, it's an effective way to get their message out.

To tap into their customer information, Del Monte and MarketTools created a social network called "Dogs are People Too" from which they determine customer opinions about their Kibbles 'n Bits and Milk-Bone products. Information from this network helped them home in on the trend to treat dogs as family members and celebrate holidays and mealtimes with their pets. This was a more effective way to garner information than to run expensive focus groups.

Mobile Marketing

The mobile web refers to the fact that, these days, people can get web access on their cell phone, PDA, or iPhone anywhere they go. The Mobile Marketing Association predicts that by 2008, 89 percent of brands will use mobile messaging to reach customers.

What are the benefits of using mobile communications? You can:

- update customers on promotions wherever they are
- build community by staying in constant touch
- provide mobile ads in context

With specific regard to texting (sending text messages to your customers on their mobile device), one of the main benefits is that you can send messages at a specific time and get immediate feedback on the results. This can be especially powerful for local businesses that have time specific events, like a fair or a store promotion.

The latest studies indicate that the audience for text messages is not limited to teens. Some findings show that the audience for texting is in the age group of thirteen to forty-five. If this is your audience, you may want to look into it. The key is to make sure that your customers can opt in and out of receiving your messages.

Chapter

Collaboration with Colleagues and Customers

No one wants advice, only collaboration.
                        —*John Steinbeck*

- ▶ **Colleagues and Customers**
- ▶ **Joint Ventures**
- ▶ **Collaboration with Customers**

Congratulations—you've created your 7 Step Action Plan. You know who you're targeting and what your message is! You've developed your company stories and know what keywords you're going to use. Once you put the 7 Step Action Plan in place, you should have a steady flow of people interested in you and your business.

Each of the online marketing tactics you choose to implement will make it easier for customers to buy from you. You put interesting information and valuable offers into your system, and customers seek you out. Next, you need to expand your reach to include new topics and new partners.

Colleagues and Customers

When you are looking at collaboration, you have two different avenues to consider. The first is partnering with colleagues—joint ventures. The second is the collaboration you do with your customers. These are two different paths, with different but equally important benefits.

Now let's look at how you can turn some of the tactics we've discussed into joint venture and community opportunities to expand your reach.

Blogs

As we've seen, a blog is one of the tactics you can use to effectively communicate with customers. It's the ideal place to float new ideas and try new things. The people who read your blog are interested in your topic and what you have to say about it. This makes it a great place to mine for new product or marketing ideas. It also lets potential joint venture partners find you.

Here are some suggestions for expanding the reach of your blog:

- **Interviews**—find experts in your field who are not widely known to the public and interview them. There are plenty of experts on the Web, not all of whom are skilled at PR. Think about the people you get your information from. Give them a chance to be heard. Your blog will be regarded as a place where new information can be found and interesting dialogue results.
- **Guest blogging**—let someone whose advice you respect do some guest blogging for you. It will give your blog some new life and might bring you a new partnership for an e-book or product offering.

- **Create an online conference**—take the leadership role and get several bloggers together to create an online conference. Sell tickets and create new products to support it. You can do the entire conference online and establish an annual one if it's successful.

Sponsorships

Consider buying advertising in someone else's newsletter to test whether the audience is one that is receptive to your message. I've tried this several times, sometimes to test a negative assumption. If I believe an audience is probably not right for me, but I'm not completely sure, I'll do a small ad test. If you find it is a receptive audience, ask the person who writes the newsletter if they'd like to partner on a small project with you. You can also offer to sponsor other people's videos and podcasts. If you know about something that's likely to go viral, you may want to add your name to the list of those associated with it as a sponsor. Of course, it needs to be an audience that is receptive to your message.

Volunteering

This is a great opportunity to do some good and learn something in the process. Find a cause you are passionate about and volunteer to help an organization that supports that cause. Once you are inside the organization, you can help them create an information e-book, develop a forum, or help them do something they hadn't considered to get more information out into the community about them. Learning something and helping spread the word about an important charity is payment enough.

CASE STUDY: Help where there's need

John Wood's volunteering story is inspiring. He was a marketing director at Microsoft and felt burned-out and in need of a vacation. He decided to visit Nepal to find respite from his daily grind. Instead, he found a library for children that had no books in it. He became inspired to bring books back for the children and decided to create a book drive. This activity proved unsuccessful because people were skeptical that a full-time Microsoft employee had the time to devote to a cause. After bringing books back with the help of his father, he decided to quit his job and set up "Room to Read," an organization devoted to creating libraries and schools for impoverished children. By the end of 2007 he created over five thousand libraries and four hundred schools. You can read about his adventure in his book Leaving Microsoft to Change the World: An Entrepreneur's Odyssey to Educate the World's Children.

Training and Mentoring

Training and mentoring are great ways to learn about marketing opportunities and find new ideas on which to collaborate with other businesses.

• Teaching others

When you are teaching others in a teleseminar or other training venue, you will very likely find new ideas and other people to network with. The other teachers who have been invited could be very valuable contacts.

• Mentoring other small business owners

If you are in a position to help other business owners from a mentoring perspective, you'll definitely learn more about how to train and what the stumbling blocks are. Then you can seek out partners for your new training plans.

Joint Ventures

On the Web, joint venturing is essential for small business owners. Some business owners use it to great advantage by working with other small businesses to do time-limited or very targeted promotions to find new customers. These promotions aren't cost-effective for a small business to do on their own, but can be very beneficial if two go in on it together. Unfortunately, most businesses don't enter into joint ventures. They fear that their customers will stop buying their products and turn to their partners instead.

Here are some important things to consider about joint ventures:

1. **You should be partnering with companies who have complimentary offerings.** If you're Pepsi, you're not partnering with Coca-Cola. But, you can partner with another food company. If you are holding off looking into joint ventures until you have an ongoing plan in place, forget it. The time to do a joint venture is when the opportunity presents itself and looks right. It extends your reach and introduces your product or service to new customers.

2. **People buy more than one item in a category.** The Web is loaded with lots of products in your selling category. If you're interested in cooking, you can learn from more than one teacher, buy books in several styles, and watch cooking shows hosted by different chefs. You know who your direct competitors are. Chances are there are very few companies that do exactly what you do. Find a company in the same realm as yours whose products compliment your own.

3. **Everyone needs fresh content to share with his or her customers.** If your content is getting stale, you need to find ways to revive it. Your partners are in the same boat. Collaborating on something can ignite your creativity.

4. **You need to develop new products.** Your customers can't buy from you a second time unless you have other items to choose from. A company with just one product will always slice the product to sell in a variety of ways. You can add a new dimension or feature to an existing product, bundle other products with it, or add updated information, but you have to do something to fulfill the ongoing needs of your customers.

5. **Joint ventures on the Web can be discrete and short-term.** If you do a small collaboration, you can test your ideas, see if your partners are worthy of your trust, and see if your customers respond. Don't go into something big with another company unless you've made small tests that have had no negative consequences. On the Web, joint ventures are defined differently than those talked about in business schools. They might involve a teaming of two partners to present a teleseminar package together, or one group reselling the other's product for a fee. If you choose your partners wisely there should be little risk.

Collaboration with Customers

Collaboration with those in your own online community provides you and your customers with several benefits that an unaffiliated social network does not, such as:

- Customers will most likely buy what they help design—if they see their suggestion in your finished product, they will buy it and spread WOM.
- It builds loyalty to your company, not just the category of product.
- It benefits all your customers by providing feedback for improvements.
- It makes participants feel like experts.
- It gives you the opportunity to reward participants with product perks.

Benefits of Customer Collaboration

In their book, *We Are Smarter Than Me: How to Unleash the Power of Crowds in Your Business*, Barry Libert and Jon Spector have lots of interesting examples of how companies benefit from collaborating with customers, such as:

- Ideas for new products
- Improved customer service
- Sales boost
- Everyone is a leader and feels invested in the product, which makes for good WOM
- Make you more productive, profitable, and makes your company a better place to work

There are many ways to collaborate with customers. I recommend that you start slow by listening to their feedback and letting them suggest improvements to you. On the far end of the spectrum is "crowdsourcing" from which you find serious contributors amidst your customers and pay them for their work.

The greatest benefit you derive when you let customers work along with you is that they become increasingly loyal. Also, they are likely to buy and recommend products in which they have a vested interest.

Chapter  19

Tracking Your Success

You always pass failure on the way to success.
—Mickey Rooney

▶ **Why You Need a Tracking System**
▶ **Timing is Everything**

You've done the work of analyzing your business and putting together your action plan—now the real fun begins. You can see how successful your online efforts are by monitoring what's written about you. The whole point of generating and following what's written is to learn and build on it. You want to continually increase customer awareness and find ways to get a jump on the competition.

Why You Need a Tracking System

As we've discussed, users can express opinions, rate your products, and influence your brand's position. If everyone writes positive things about your company, life is great. But, if you have a disgruntled customer fairly expressing a problem they've encountered, you want to know about it so you can fix it. Negative feedback can be much more valuable than positive.

It's important to monitor negative feedback, but it's equally important to monitor how your current tactics are working. You know you're getting traffic from your blog, your websites, ads, etc. But wouldn't looking at the actual opinions and thoughts of your customers as they move around your sites be invaluable? That's what a monitoring system can help you do. You also want to track what's being said about you to monitor your reputation.

Setting up your tracking system

With all the web tools available today to capture this information, it's easy to set up your tracking system. But it requires some thought to make it really useful. Obviously, you need to decide what information will be helpful to you. Don't feel you have to track ten different concepts when one or two are sufficient.

Aside from your own web analytics, you also want to track other people's blogs, discussion forums, Google searches, Yahoo, etc. If you feel you are lacking information in a particular area, check out sources like the Web 2.0 Top 1,000 list at www.web20searchengine.com/web20/web-2.0-list.htm to see what new tools have been developed.

To create a good working list of things to track, ask yourself these questions:

- What company names will I track?
- What are the product names and/or service names I want to track?
- What are the names of the people I want to track inside the company (remember to include yourself and employees with a high profile)?
- What are the names of the high profile people in my industry that I want to track?
- What are the concepts and trends I want to track?
- Who are the competitors I want to track?

QUICK Tip

Technorati: If you were only going to track information from one site (which is not advisable), it should be Technorati.com. It is hands down the most used blog search engine in the world. You should make sure to "claim your blog" on the site so that you are among the almost 110 million blogs tracked in 2007. Reading and searching on Technorati give you a good idea about what topics are important on the Web. Make sure to create specific topic searches so you can track what's being said.

Here are ten good ways to keep up with news about your company and trends that may affect it:

1. Start Pages

If you want to collect all your information from one screen, I recommend that you begin with what is called a "start page." Start pages allow you to collect different types of information in one place—think "personal portal." I use www.NetVibes.com and www.Google.com/ig as my start pages. Netvibes lets you set up as many searches as you want and has search engines preselected. If you already have a Google Gmail account, then iGoogle would make sense. If you like to have all the information you want about what's going on in one place, try a start page.

2. Feed Readers

If you want to collect similar types of information **from one screen**, you'll need a feed reader to grab the feeds you want. (In this section, we're looking at feed readers to collect information for tracking purposes. For a more extensive discussion of feed readers, check Chapter 5: You're a Publisher Now!) I use www.Bloglines.com to collect a majority of the blogs I read in one place. It's also linked to my Typepad blog so that if I want, I can automatically add a blog to my blogroll. www.NewsGator.com is another good one-page system for collecting information of the same type on one screen.

3. Alerts

You want to sign up for Google alerts at www.Google.com/alerts so that you can automatically monitor when your keywords are mentioned. If you prefer, Yahoo has one at Alerts.Yahoo.com.

4. Specific Page Updates

If you need to watch specific web pages to see when they are updated, try www.Watchthatpage.com and www.Trackengine.com. (Note: If you own the advanced professional version of Copernic Agent, mentioned in Chapter 4 it does a good job of tracking pages.)

5. Search Across Social Networks

Several engines have sprung up to find names across social networks. If you need to do this, try www.Yoname.com or www.Wink.com. By tracking the names of influential people in your business, you can see if they are participating or recommending new things.

6. Word-of-Mouth

www.Serph.com and www.Omigli.com are great places to search when you want to find user-generated content about your products or services. Make sure to sort by date and you can see what customers are saying everyday.

7. Rankings

Popular tools you can use to track your own ranking are www.Alexa.com and www.Icerocket.com.

8. Forums, Message Boards

These two help you find out what's being said on forums and message boards—www.boardreader.com and www.bigboards.com.

9. Groups

These two have been around a long time and help you find out what's being said about your products in organized groups—groups.google.com and groups.yahoo.com.

10. Trend Tracking

As we mentioned in the WOM section, you want to keep abreast of what's happening in the marketplace so that you are alerted to new things that impact your customer's thinking. Besides subscribing to newsletters and blogs in your industry, try these tools to keep abreast of new trends and ideas:

- www.Hitwise.com
- www.Google.com/trends
- www.buzz.yahoo.com
- www.trendwatching.com
- www.m-trends.org
- www.marketingcharts.com
- www.blogpulse.com

Timing is Everything

In 2007, *Inc.* magazine published an interesting guest column by Ray Kurzweil, called "How to Predict the Future." Kurzweil, considered by some as the heir apparent to Edison, developed the Kurzweil Reading Machine to assist the blind. The machine scans readable text and speaks it so that the sight-impaired can hear what's on the screen.

Kurzweil is also known for being ready with other new inventions just when the market starts to grow. While other people are scrambling to create a product, he has already put in the years of development and can offer a working product. This is a great skill to have and one that all small business owners and entrepreneurs would love to possess.

He made it clear that he doesn't possess psychic abilities. Kurzweil believes that a good sense of timing is the key to his success. He points to the fact that "an inclination to project the current rate of change into the future is hard-wired in us." This causes us to assume that our ability to create something new is based on how long it takes us to create something new right now. A look at the dramatic speed with which the Internet changes certainly proves this to be a false assumption.

So what can you do to make meaningful predictions? The method he uses is a good one for small business owners who live or die by their business projections. Two mindset changes are critical:

- Internet tools change so fast that you need to understand that a three-year prediction will miss new technology developments. Did you foresee your business blog driving traffic two years ago? If you are working on a new technology, make sure you plan to deliver it in less than three years.
- The problems that you worry about today may be solved more quickly than you expect. The best way to guide your small online business is to make short plans that get re-evaluated often. This is why I always use three-month projections in my business.

Alert!

Everything Changes: Intuit founder Scott Cook holds fast to the notion that business today holds very different lessons for its leaders. In an interview in the September 2007 issue of *Inc.* Magazine, he is quoted as saying, "any leader today had better get used to being surprised at having things you thought to be true turn out not to be true." You need to remain open-minded and be prepared to take advantage of an opportunity when it presents itself.

CASE STUDY: Three questions for Mike Bell, veteran software entrepreneur

1. Mike, what one tip would you give to business people just getting started online?

Validate your concept and its assumptions before you race to expand. Many entrepreneurs focus so much effort on going big fast that they often race right by the question of whether their business idea is on-target. Even the brightest entrepreneur with a model aimed at sound logic can be wrong—in big ways or small. Very few of us hit the bulls-eye on the first shot. And there is absolutely nothing wrong with this. It's a natural part of the entrepreneurial process and of growing a business. But racing ahead towards growth and expansion should come only after a deliberate learning phase.

2. What social media tactics are in the forefront for Software.com?

User reviews on steroids. Collecting and disseminating candid, uncensored user feedback has quickly become a rote function for commerce sites. It is a fundamental requirement—not a differentiator. My team and I are working on the next generation of user feedback that makes this information more targeted and demographically segmented, and better compiled—qualities that ultimately make them more useful to consumers.

3. What is the one tip you would give anyone planning to use user-generated content as a marketing tactic?

Don't censor it and find a way to take it one step further.

Additional resources: Mike Bell is currently working on growing Software.com into the world's leading software marketplace, as its CEO and founder. You can reach Mike at: mike@software.com

Afterword

There is an old saying that states, "An expert knows the answers if you ask the right questions." I think the key to growing an online business is asking the right questions.

I have tried to pack this book with many questions you can ask yourself along the way. Framing the right question makes everything easier. When you are working on a problem, think long and hard about what the real question is that you are trying to answer.

For example, "How can I find new customers to visit my website?" is a much more productive question than "How can I fit a newsletter into my online strategy?" If you conclude from asking the first question that a newsletter is the right tactic, then you have helped your business move forward. By asking the second question, you are making assumptions that may be incorrect. Continue to refine your questions and you will have a thriving business.

Appendix

Bibliography

Books Cited by Chapter

Chapter 1
Anderson, Chris. *The Long Tail: Why the Future of Business is Selling Less of More*. New York: Hyperion, 2006.

Godin, Seth. *Permission Marketing: Turning Strangers Into Friends And Friends Into Customers*. New York: Simon & Schuster, 1999.

Levine, Rick, Christopher Locke, Doc Searls, and David Weinberger. *The Cluetrain Manifesto: The End of Business as Usual*. Reading: Perseus Books, 2001.

Chapter 2
Maeda, John. *The Laws of Simplicity*. Cambridge, MA: MIT Press, 2006.

Chapter 3
Buzan, Tony, with Barry Buzan. *The Mind Map Book: How to Use Radiant Thinking to Maximize Your Brain's Untapped Potential*. New York: Plume Book, 1996.

Galenson, David. *Old Masters and Young Geniuses: The Two Life Cycles of Artistic Creativity*. Princeton, NJ: Princeton University Press, 2006.

Kanter, Rosabeth Moss. *Confidence: How Winning Streaks and Losing Streaks Begin and End*. New York: Crown Business, 2004.

Miller, Anne. *Metaphorically Selling*. New York: Chiron Associates, 2004.

Pink, Daniel. *A Whole New Mind: Moving from the Information Age to the Conceptual Age*. New York: Berkeley, 2005.

Pressfield, Steven. *The War of Art: Break Through the Blocks and Win Your Inner Creative Battles*. New York: Warner Books, 2002.

Toffler, Alvin, and Heidi Toffler. *Revolutionary Wealth: How it will be created and how it will change our lives*. Sydney: Currency, 2007.

Tharp, Twyla. *The Creative Habit: Learn It and Use It for Life*. New York: Simon & Schuster, 2005.

Chapter 4

Bayan, Richard. *More Words that Sell*. New York: McGraw-Hill, 2003.

Godin, Seth. *All Marketers Are Liars: The Power of Telling Authentic Stories in a Low-Trust World*. New York: Portfolio, 2005.

Werz, Edward, and Sally Germain. *Phrases that Sell: The Ultimate Phrase Finder to Help You Promote Your Products, Services, and Ideas*. Chicago: Contemporary Books, 1998.

Chapter 6

Goto, Kelly, and Emily Cotler. *Web Redesign 2.0: Workflow that Works*. Indianapolis: New Riders, 2005.

Krug, Steve. *Don't Make Me Think: A Common Sense Approach to Web Usability*. Indianapolis: New Riders, 2005.

Nielsen, Jakob. *Designing Web Usability*. Indianapolis: New Riders, 1999.

Chapter 8

Cooper, Alan. *The Inmates are Running the Asylum: Why High Tech Products Drive Us Crazy and How to Restore the Sanity*. Indianapolis: SAMS, 2004.

Chapter 9

Ries, Al, and Jack Trout. *Positioning: The Battle for Your Mind*. New York: McGraw-Hill, 1981.

Trout, Jack, with Steve Rivkin. *The New Positioning: The Latest on the World's #1 Business Strategy*. New York: McGraw-Hill, 1996.

Chapter 10

Atkinson, Cliff. *Beyond Bullet Points: Using Microsoft Powerpoint to Create Presentations That Inform, Motivate, and Inspire*. Redmond: Microsoft Press, 2005.

Boettinger, Henry. *Moving Mountains or The Art and Craft of Letting Others See Things Your Way*. London: Macmillan, 1969.

Heath, Chip, and Dan Heath. *Made to Stick: Why Some Ideas Survive and Others Die*. New York: Random House, 2007.

Loehr, Jim. *The Power of Story: Rewrite Your Destiny in Business and in Life*. New York: Free Press, 2007.

Simmons, Annette. *The Story Factor: Inspiration, Influence, And Persuasion Through the Art of Stories*. Cambridge, MA: Perseus Pub, 2001.

Chapter 12

Cialdini, Robert. *Influence: How and Why People Agree to Things*. New York: Morrow, 1984.

Sanders, Tim. *The Likeability Factor: How to Boost Your L Factor and Achieve Your Life's Dreams*. New York: Crown, 2005.

Chapter 14

Stelzner, Michael A. *Writing White Papers: How to Capture Readers and Keep Them Engaged*. Poway, CA: WhitePaperSource Publishing, 2007.

Chapter 17

Gladwell, Malcolm. *The Tipping Point: How Little Things Can Make a Big Difference*. Boston: Little, Brown, 2000.

Kawasaki, Guy. *The Art of the Start: The Time-Tested, Battle-Hardened Guide for Anyone Starting Anything*. New York: Portfolio, 2004.

Keller, Edward, and Jon Berry. *The Influentials: One American in Ten Tells the Other Nine How to Vote, Where to Eat, and What to Buy*. New York: Free Press, 2003.

Chapter 18

Libert, Barry, and Jon Spector. *We Are Smarter than Me: How to Unleash the Power of Crowds in Your Business*. Upper Saddle River, NJ: Wharton School Publishing, 2007.

Wood, John. *Leaving Microsoft to Change the World: An Entrepreneur's Odyssey to Educate the World's Children*. London: Collins, 2006.

Tools by Chapter

Chapter 3
MindManager 7 Software
   www.mindjet.com/us/download/

Chapter 4
Highlight and clip web content
   www.ilighter.com
Specialized Searching
   www.copernic.com/en/products/agent/download.html
   www.topicseekers.com
Freelancers
   www.elance.com

Chapter 5
Feed Burners
   www.Feedburner.com
   www.Feedblitz.com
   www.Feedforall.com
Content Aggregators
   www.netvibes.com
Spam Filter
   http://spamassassin.apache.org/
Widgets
   http://widgets.yahoo.com
   http://desktop.google.com/plugins/
Free Conference Calls service
   www.Freeconferencecall.com
   www.Freeconference.com
Autoresponder/Mailing Lists
   www.1ShoppingCart.com
   www.AWeber.com

Chapter 6
Graphical Website Editor
   www.adobe.com/products/contribute/

Chapter 11
Keyword Suggestion Tools
   http://inventory.overture.com/d/searchinventory/suggestion/
   http://wordtracker.com

Chapter 13
Blogging Platforms
   www.typepad.com
   www.wordpress.com
Resources
   www.problogger.net/archives/2006/04/15/blog-tools/
   www.masternewmedia.org/rss/top55/
Microblogging
   www.twitter.com
   www.pownce.com
Podcasting
   www.AudioAcrobat.com
   http://audacity.sourceforge.net/
Professional Networks
   General Business www.LinkedIn.com
   Medicine www.md.sermo.com
   Real Estate www.Activerain.com
   Advertising www.AdGabber.com
Social Networks
   www.Facebook.com
   www.MySpace.com
Online Community Tools
   www.Ning.com
   www.Squidoo.com

Wikis
  www.PDWiki.com
  www.editme.com
Social Bookmarking and Tagging
  www.del.icio.us
  www.Digg.com
  www.Stumbleupon.com
Customer Reviews
  www.consumersearch.com
  www.epinions.com

Chapter 14

Email Service Providers
  www.constantcontact.com
www.1shoppingcart.com
  www.exacttarget.com
Article Marketing Services
  www.ezinearticles.com
  www.articlemarketer.com
Online Press Releases
  www.businesswire.com
  www.prnewswire.com
  www.prweb.com
Press Platform
  www.expertclick.com/brochure
Online Polls
  Website: www.surveymonkey.com
  Blogs: www.vizu.com
        www.blogpolls.com

Chapter 15
Website Analytics
   www.google.com/analytics
Dead Link Checker
   www.dead-links.com/check_links.php

Chapter 19
Start Pages
   www.NetVibes.com
   www.Google.com/ig
Feed Readers
   www.Bloglines.com
   www.newsgator.com
Alerts
   www.Google.com/alerts
   alerts.Yahoo.com
Specific Page Updates
   www.Watchthatpage.com
   www.Trackengine.com
Search social networks for names
   www.Yoname.com
   www.Wink.com
Word-of-Mouth
   www.Serph.com
   www.Omigli.com
Rankings
   www.Alexa.com
   www.Icerocket.com
Forums, Message Boards
   www.boardreader.com
   www.bigboards.com
Groups
   groups.google.com/
   groups.yahoo.com/

Trend Tracking
   www.Hitwise.com
   www.Google.com/trends
   www.buzz.yahoo.com
   www.trendwatching.com
   www.m-trends.org
   www.marketingcharts.com/
   www.blogpulse.com

Appendix  B

Worksheets

WEBSITE ASSESSMENT QUIZ

To find out if your website is ready for an overhaul, please answer yes or no to the following nine questions:

1. Has the size of your website site grown substantially in the last year?

   YES _____ **NO**_____

2. Is 25 percent or more of the content outdated or unnecessary?

   YES _____ **NO**_____

3. Do users have to click more than twice to buy something?

   YES _____ **NO**_____

4. Are you procrastinating about using social media marketing tactics on your site? (e.g., share this page)

   YES _____ **NO**_____

5. Does your website design reflect old business objectives—not what you are focusing on now?

   YES _____ **NO**_____

6. Do you have "one size fits all" content for everyone who visits your site?

   YES _____ **NO**_____

7. Do your headlines and copy talk about features and not benefits?

   YES _____ **NO**_____

8. Are your pages so chock full of content that they're hard to read?

   YES _____ **NO**_____

9. Are you reluctant to determine how visitors use your site, so you don't look at any web statistics?

   YES _____ **NO**_____

WEBSITE ASSESSMENT QUIZ ANSWERS

Once you have filled out the worksheet, let's look at what the answers mean to you.

1. If you answered yes to **ALL** the items on your worksheet, work your way through the steps in order: Navigation in Chapter 6; Content in Chapter 12; Tactics in Chapters 13 and 14; and Web Analytics in Chapter 15.

2. If you answered yes to items one, two, seven, and eight, your first focus should be on **Content (Chapter 12)**.

   Within a short time of launch, I'm sure you'll notice that your website is growing—more pages; more content. You start to see where the content holes are and what information your customers are asking for that you haven't supplied.

   Within a year, however, the site may start to look and feel like a patchwork quilt. This doesn't mean you are doing anything wrong, but it does require some action. Your business is taking shape and changing to suit the environment and your customers. Unless you make an effort to reorganize and refine, your website will not be as effective and profitable as it could be.

   If you answered yes to items three and five, your first focus should be on **Navigation and Design (Chapter 6)**.

   It's important for users to find everything they need to make a buying decision. As your business grows, your objectives may change and your product mix will change too. You need to focus on how easy it is to buy and how you can make it effortless.

   If you answered yes to items four and six, your first focus should be on **Tactics (Chapters 13 and 14)**. I've presented a host of tactics, both new and tried and true, that will help you increase business.

   If you answered yes to question nine, your first focus should be on **Web Analytics (Chapter 15)**. I firmly believe that you can't really make useful changes to your website if you can't determine how visitors are using it now. Make sure you read that chapter to see how web analytics can make a big difference.

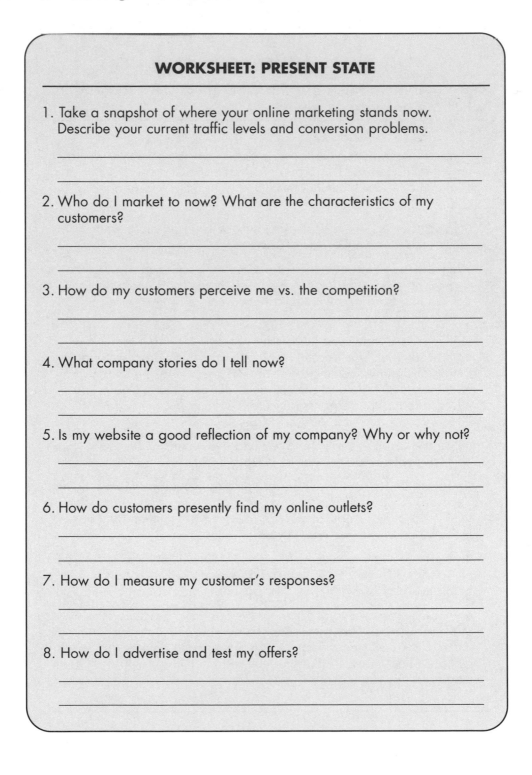

WORKSHEET: PRESENT STATE

1. Take a snapshot of where your online marketing stands now. Describe your current traffic levels and conversion problems.

   _____

   _____

2. Who do I market to now? What are the characteristics of my customers?

   _____

   _____

3. How do my customers perceive me vs. the competition?

   _____

   _____

4. What company stories do I tell now?

   _____

   _____

5. Is my website a good reflection of my company? Why or why not?

   _____

   _____

6. How do customers presently find my online outlets?

   _____

   _____

7. How do I measure my customer's responses?

   _____

   _____

8. How do I advertise and test my offers?

   _____

   _____

WORKSHEET: PRESENT MINDSET

1. What social media tactics and tools do I use today?

   _____

   _____

2. Do I try to inject innovation and creativity to my business today? If so, how?

   _____

   _____

3. When I write online content, do I use any specific copywriting rules or guidelines?

   _____

   _____

4. Do my customers help me shape my marketing message?

   _____

   _____

5. Do I let users provide their own product reviews, comments, or videos?

   _____

   _____

LANDING PAGE WORKSHEET

1. What is the ONE action you want your customer to take after reading your landing page?

   _____

   _____

2. Does your landing page match the ad that precedes it? Will the reader make the necessary connection between what the ad said and how it looks with the landing page content? Why?

   _____

   _____

3. What does the design of your landing page say to the reader?

   _____

   _____

4. Have you removed all extraneous links from the landing page and just included the few powerful ones?

   _____

   _____

5. Is your call to action clear?

   _____

   _____

6. How are you going to measure the results from your landing page campaign?

   _____

   _____

CONCLUSIONS WORKSHEET—STEP 1. NICHE

1. Describe your niche audience's demographics in one sentence.

_____

_____

2. Describe your niche audience's psychographics.

_____

_____

3. Describe your perfect customer in detail.

_____

_____

4. What groups will you create for your mailing list?

_____

_____

5. List the personas you have created and give the characteristics for each.

_____

_____

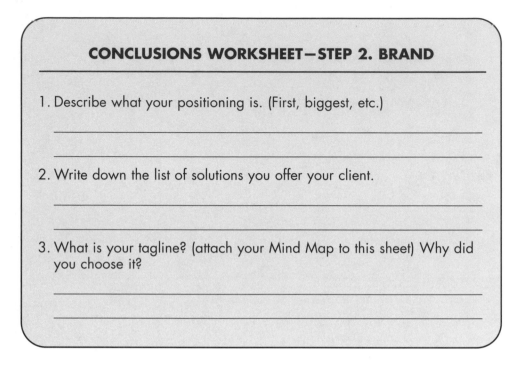

CONCLUSIONS WORKSHEET—STEP 2. BRAND

1. Describe what your positioning is. (First, biggest, etc.)

_____

_____

2. Write down the list of solutions you offer your client.

_____

_____

3. What is your tagline? (attach your Mind Map to this sheet) Why did you choose it?

_____

_____

CONCLUSIONS WORKSHEET—STEP 3. STORY

1. Describe one story that you want everyone associated with your company to tell. Which of the three plots does it contain—challenge, connection, creativity?

   _____

   _____

2. Develop a story about why you created your business. Which of the three plots does it contain—challenge, connection, creativity?

   _____

   _____

3. List some of the metaphors you will be using.

   _____

   _____

4. How do plan to capture success stories?

   _____

   _____

CONCLUSIONS WORKSHEET—STEP 4. SEARCH

1. What are the words you brainstormed for your keyword list? (Keep a record of all of them in case you want to revisit them.)

_____

_____

2. What are the goals you have for SEO?

_____

_____

3. What are the keywords for each niche?

_____

_____

4. Which keyword suggestion tool did you use?

_____

_____

5. What keywords are your competitors using?

_____

_____

CONCLUSIONS WORKSHEET—STEP 5. CONTENT

1. Do you have adequate information for each of your four content "must-haves?" (About Us, Support and contact, Help and FAQs, Press Room)

   _____

   _____

2. Have you analyzed your content to ensure that you don't make the three beginner's mistakes? What did you find?

   _____

   _____

3. Did you fill out the Landing Page Worksheet? Are you satisfied with it?

   _____

   _____

4. Will you use a sales letter? Did you create the content?

   _____

   _____

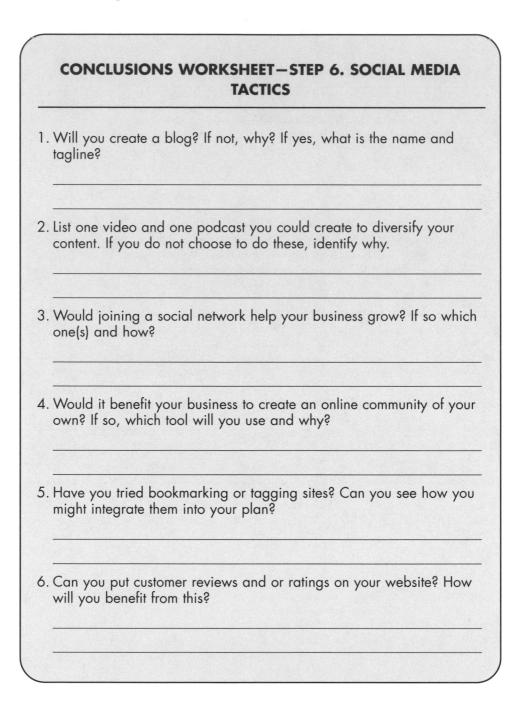

CONCLUSIONS WORKSHEET—STEP 6. SOCIAL MEDIA TACTICS

1. Will you create a blog? If not, why? If yes, what is the name and tagline?

   _____

   _____

2. List one video and one podcast you could create to diversify your content. If you do not choose to do these, identify why.

   _____

   _____

3. Would joining a social network help your business grow? If so which one(s) and how?

   _____

   _____

4. Would it benefit your business to create an online community of your own? If so, which tool will you use and why?

   _____

   _____

5. Have you tried bookmarking or tagging sites? Can you see how you might integrate them into your plan?

   _____

   _____

6. Can you put customer reviews and or ratings on your website? How will you benefit from this?

   _____

   _____

CONCLUSIONS WORKSHEET—STEP 6. TRIED AND TRUE TACTICS

1. Have you completed the article marketing steps? Do you have a plan created to produce articles? Describe it.

   _____

   _____

2. Would a newsletter benefit you at this time? If so, do you have a tool picked out? If not, why?

   _____

   _____

3. How could press releases benefit you now? If you're waiting, why?

   _____

   _____

4. Do you have white papers written? Would they benefit you? If so, how will you get them written?

   _____

   _____

5. Can you survey or create a poll to learn more about your audience? If so, what tool and what topic?

   _____

   _____

6. Are you thinking about other tactics like loyalty programs, affiliate programs, speaking engagements, joint ventures, and postcards? If so, which ones and how will you take the next step to create them? Make sure to list the tools you will use.

   _____

   _____

CONCLUSIONS WORKSHEET—STEP 7. RESULTS

1. Have you used web analytics in the past? If not, why not?

   _____

   _____

2. List the benefits you'll get from using web analytics now.

   _____

   _____

3. Which tool will you use for your web analytics? Is it set up? If not, how will you get it set up?

   _____

   _____

4. What measures will you track? List at least five.

   _____

   _____

5. Which other marketing channels will you track, like your blog, newsletter, etc.?

   _____

   _____

TIME VS. REVENUE ASSESSMENT

1. Start by listing the five activities that bring in the most revenue on a monthly basis. These could be products, ad revenue, royalties, consulting fees, etc.

    1. _____

    2. _____

    3. _____

    4. _____

    5. _____

2. List the five activities that bring you the most traffic. These could be blogs, newsletters, social networking, etc.

    1. _____

    2. _____

    3. _____

    4. _____

    5. _____

3. Of those that generate traffic, which ones can you definitively say translate into direct revenue?

    1. _____

    2. _____

    3. _____

    4. _____

    5. _____

4. Of those that don't generate direct revenue, which ones have the most potential to generate direct revenue?

   1. _____

   2. _____

   3. _____

   4. _____

   5. _____

5. Which activities do I spend time on that have no potential to generate revenue or support revenue generation?

   1. _____

   2. _____

   3. _____

   4. _____

   5. _____

NEW MINDSET WORKSHEET

1. What social media tactics and tools do I plan to use?

   _____

   _____

2. Which direct mail copywriting rules or guidelines will I use?

   _____

   _____

3. What User-Generated Content can I use to get feedback from customers?

   _____

   _____

4. Are there new ways I plan to collaborate online with employees or partners?

   _____

   _____

5. Who is on my targeted list of influencers?

   _____

   _____

6. Do I have any new ideas about how to innovate?

   _____

   _____

WORKSHEET—YOUR 7 STEP PLAN COMPLETE

1. Describe in detail one or several segmented target audiences that you will market to. (Define target markets)

   _____

   _____

2. How are you positioning your company? Do you have a tagline for it? How will customers think about your brand? (Define your position)

   _____

   _____

3. What is your company's story? (Develop your story)

   _____

   _____

4. List the types of content formats you will provide online (e.g., podcast, video). (Website Content)

   _____

   _____

5. What is the search strategy that makes it easy for your customer to find you? (What tools, what keywords, etc.) (Keywords and Search Engines)

   _____

   _____

6. What tactics have you chosen (both social media and tried and true) to generate more revenue? (Tactics)

   _____

   _____

7. What measurements will you use to analyze actions taken by customers? (Results)

   _____

   _____

Index

Shelton State Libraries
Shelton State Community College

About the Author

Stephanie Diamond is a thought leader and management/marketing professional with twenty-five years of experience building profits in a broad range of product and service businesses. She is a frequent commentator and author on the topics of digital marketing, product development, e-commerce, project management, and operations.

She worked for eight years as Marketing Director at AOL. When she joined AOL there were fewer than 1 million subscribers. When she left in 2002 there were 36 million. As she likes to say, "A lot happened to the Internet in between." She created a highly successful line of multimedia software products that sold millions of copies for AOL and has developed unique business strategies and products for a variety of companies. She has worked for such media companies as Redgate New Media, Newsweek, Inc., and AOL Time Warner.

In 2002, she founded Digital Media Works, Inc., a marketing consultancy and design firm. She is passionate about helping online companies successfully focus their tactics and grow their businesses.

As a strategic thinker, Stephanie uses mind-mapping techniques originally developed by Tony Buzan to develop creative solutions that take companies to the next level. She writes a monthly online column for Mindjet that presents solutions for marketers using custom maps.

Stephanie received a BA in psychology from Hofstra University and an MSW and MPH from the University of Hawaii. She lives in New York with her husband and an eleven-year-old Maltese named Tyler.

To download copies of book worksheets, assessments, bonuses, discounts, and free information and to find out more about how Stephanie Diamond can help grow your business, please go to www.webmarketingforsmallbusinesses.com